THE POWER OF UNSTOPPABLE
MOMENTUM

Key Drivers to **REVOLUTIONIZE** Your District

MICHAEL FULLAN
MARK A. EDWARDS

Solution Tree | Press
a division of
Solution Tree

555 North Morton Street
Bloomington, IN 47404
800.733.6786 (toll free) / 812.336.7700
FAX: 812.336.7790

email: info@SolutionTree.com
SolutionTree.com
Printed in the United States of America

21 20 19 18 17   2 3 4 5

Library of Congress Cataloging-in-Publication Data

Names: Fullan, Michael. | Edwards, Mark A.
Title: The power of unstoppable momentum : key drivers to revolutionize your
    district / Michael Fullan, Mark A. Edwards.
Description: Bloomington, IN : Solution Tree Press, [2017] | Includes
    bibliographical references and index.
Identifiers: LCCN 2017007869 | ISBN 9781942496557 (perfect bound)
Subjects: LCSH: School improvement programs--United States. | School
    districts--United States. | School management and organization--United
    States. | School superintendents--United States. | Educational
    technology--United States.
Classification: LCC LB2822.82 .F854 2017 | DDC 371.2/07--dc23 LC record
available at https://lccn.loc.gov/2017007869

Solution Tree
Jeffrey C. Jones, CEO
Edmund M. Ackerman, President

Solution Tree Press
President and Publisher: Douglas M. Rife
Editorial Director: Sarah Payne-Mills
Managing Production Editor: Caroline Cascio
Senior Production Editor: Todd Brakke
Senior Editor: Amy Rubenstein
Copy Editor: Evie Madsen
Proofreader: Elisabeth Abrams
Cover Designer: Rian Anderson
Editorial Assistants: Jessi Finn and Kendra Slayton

ACKNOWLEDGMENTS

Michael Fullan thanks the growing number of colleagues around the world working on deep learning. This is truly a global movement, and we are learning a mile a minute. You are too numerous to mention but thanks especially to those directly participating to and contributing to New Pedagogies for Deep Learning (www.npdl .global), to my direct support team, and to Solution Tree for their great work in shepherding this book into publication.

Mark A. Edwards thanks all teachers and school leaders who work every day to grow their capacity to prepare students for their future. We are building new learning trajectories for students, teachers, and school leaders that have the potential to have a positive impact in the United States and around the world. Thanks to the Solution Tree team for this opportunity.

Solution Tree Press would like to thank the following reviewers:

Corey Austin
Superintendent
Target Range School District #23
Missoula, Montana

Geoffrey Thomas
Superintendent
Madison School District 321
Rexburg, Idaho

Daniel Bittman
Superintendent
Sauk Rapids-Rice Public Schools
Sauk Rapids, Minnesota

Thomas Tucker
Superintendent
Princeton City Schools
Cincinnati, Ohio

Doug Lambert
Superintendent
Grant County Schools
Petersburg, West Virginia

TABLE OF CONTENTS

CHAPTER SEVEN

ABOUT THE AUTHORS

 **Michael Fullan, PhD,** is former dean of the Ontario Institute for Studies in Education at the University of Toronto. Recognized as an international authority on educational reform, Michael engages in training, consulting, and evaluating change projects around the world. Many countries use his ideas for managing change.

Michael helped lead the evaluation team that conducted the assessment of the National Literacy and Numeracy Strategy in England from 1998 to 2003. Later, he was appointed special adviser to the premier and minister of education in Ontario, a post that he still holds.

In December 2012, Michael received the Order of Canada, one of Canada's highest civilian honors. The Order of Canada was established in 1967 to recognize a lifetime of outstanding achievement, dedication to community, and service to the nation.

Michael bases his work on the moral purpose of education as it is applied in schools and school systems to bring about major improvements. He has written several best-selling books that have been translated into many languages. His latest books include *Leadership: Key Competencies for Whole-System Change* (with Lyle Kirtman); *The Principal: Three Keys to Maximizing Impact*; *Professional Capital: Transforming Teaching in Every School* (with Andy Hargreaves); *Freedom to Change: Four Strategies to Put Your*

Inner Drive Into Overdrive; *Coherence: The Right Drivers in Action for Schools, Districts, and Systems* (with Joanne Quinn); and *Indelible Leadership: Always Leave Them Learning.*

To learn more about Michael's work, visit www.michaelfullan.ca or follow him on Twitter @MichaelFullan1.

Mark A. Edwards, EdD, serves as senior vice president of digital learning for Discovery Education. He previously served as superintendent of the Mooresville Graded School District from 2007–2016.

Mark was named the 2013 School Superintendents Association (AASA) National Superintendent of the Year and the 2013 North Carolina Superintendent of the Year. He also served as Superintendent of Henrico County Public Schools from 1994–2004. He was named the Virginia Superintendent of the Year in 2001 and was the recipient of the Harold McGraw Prize in Education in 2003.

Mark was on the founding board of directors of the Digital Promise League of Innovative Schools and AASA's Digital Consortium. Mark received North Carolina's prestigious Order of the Long Leaf Pine Award in 2013 and the Public School Forum of North Carolina Jay Robinson Education Leadership Award in 2014.

Mark has been recognized as a pioneer in one-to-one computing and has published two books related to this work, *Every Child, Every Day: A Digital Conversion Model for Student Achievement* and *Thank You for Your Leadership: The Power of Distributed Leadership in a Digital Conversion Model.*

Follow Mark on Twitter @MarkEdw22.

To book Michael Fullan or Mark A. Edwards for professional development, contact pd@SolutionTree.com.

UNSTOPPABLE FORCES

Change is inexorable. This is not a revelatory idea, but it is essential for district leaders to understand that the change forces at work in our schools, including rapid technology development, require us to adapt our teaching practices to work in concert with these forces instead of acting as a buttress against them. Indeed, district leaders that embrace whole-system change, continually learning and adapting their district's methods to the times, better maintain long-term sustainability and accentuate all the benefits that change can bring.

Whole-system change has three core characteristics: (1) it is about changing *all the schools* in a district, state, or province and not just a few schools; (2) it always zeroes in on *changing pedagogy*—the way students learn; and (3) it always develops and traces *the causal pathways to impact on measurable student learning outcomes.*

In this book, we closely examine certain *unstoppable forces*. But that doesn't mean that such forces automatically do good things; in fact, this book is about how to harness the powerful dynamics present in our culture and convert them into beneficial, deep system changes. There are four themes underway in education that are unstoppable.

1. Traditional schooling is outdated, and students (and we think many teachers) will no longer tolerate the status quo. Boredom and alienation are big push factors.

2. Ubiquitous digital innovation, coupled with social media and other networks, no longer aligns with the hierarchy of existing governance models.

3. New modes of learning—new powerful pedagogies, if you will—are unleashing motivational forces across the spectrum of students. Indeed, we argue that the combination of new pedagogies and digital resources provides opportunities to engage historically disadvantaged students in ways heretofore impossible.

4. New forms of leadership, which we identify in this book, are bringing about positive change. Some of these forces come from the *middle*—the layer between the state or province and the local community. As the middle leverages change, we see new energy bubbling up from the bottom—from students and teachers (Fullan, 2016).

Because these unstoppable forces can create chaos and harm, our book is about how to corral and shape these forces for the common good—to help make unstoppably good things happen. One of us—Michael Fullan—has been focusing on whole-system change since 2003, working with governments and school districts and municipalities in different countries. The other—Mark A. Edwards—led a lowly funded, 50 percent poverty school district (Mooresville Graded School District [MGSD] in North Carolina) to remarkable success during the same period. Indeed, in this book we show how the MGSD has become an inspiration for other districts across the United

States. Moreover, MGSD and others are a part of a global movement toward deep learning (Fullan, Quinn, & McEachen, in press).

We are *doers*—we go from practice to research. Our commitment to action is our modus operandi. We use action as the vehicle for learning what it takes to have an impact. We then write about what we learn and do it better the next time, gaining more insights, writing more, doing more, and so on. We represent a cumulative learning process, and we are proud to share where we are in our doing and thinking in this book.

Chapter 1 raises the red flag of superficial change, or what we might call the *trap of modernity*. Although effective technology use is essential to taking advantage of today's unstoppable forces, if you mistakenly start with technology as your answer, you end up going down the wrong path. Technology is ubiquitous, but it is so easy to surround yourself digitally and not learn anything worthwhile. To dabble is to be worldwide and an inch deep.

In chapters 2–5 we take up the essence of the positive change solution. We examine what deep learning is and what makes it occur. We use our professional capital framework to show that you need all three capitals (social, human, and decisional) working in the service of deep learning (Hargreaves & Fullan, 2012). To understand *capital* in this context, think of the worth of individual and group assets and how you must leverage them to achieve broader goals. Capital is powerful when it circulates. When educators learn from each other in purposeful and innovative ways, as they do at MGSD, they are building and using professional capital in ways that improve and sustain the whole system.

Chapters 6 and 7 identify ideas for moving forward. Chapter 6 arrives at key lessons from MGSD for generating unstoppable learning. Chapter 7 goes beyond Mooresville to see how other districts generate unstoppable momentum in learning, including detailed vignettes from district leaders that detail how they reaped the benefits of whole-system change. Although much of what we write about in this book begins with our experiences at MGSD, there are three encouraging features for wider change we want to highlight.

1.   MGSD is a *very* hard case. They don't get much harder, unless you go to the giant urban districts. If they can do it, anyone can do it.

2.   MGSD did not carry out its work in isolation. From day one, the district has been a dynamic part of a movement across the United States whereby the district learned from other districts and then helped other districts learn.

3.   Other districts did learn from MGSD, and in chapter 7 we look at six other districts that are part of a network of districts going down similar paths.

We should make it crystal clear that this is not a book about technology. The driver is *deep cultural change* in how districts operate— to have measurable impacts on how and what all students learn. Pedagogy and culture are the drivers; technology is the accelerator.

Finally, we can say with confidence that any district can dramatically improve the way that MGSD did. However, a cardinal change lesson from system work is that you can never be successful by trying to replicate or imitate other successes.

We talk in this book about what factors contributed to MGSD's success, but it is not a strict model. You need to learn from other successes and then figure out a unique pathway that fits your own situation and culture. This book provides good ideas and valuable lessons, but more than anything else it is an invitation for you, the reader, to create your own constellation of unstoppable forces to generate deep and lasting change that benefits those you work with and the students and families you work for.

chapter one

LEARNING IS NOT ABOUT THE TECHNOLOGY

As of 2017, the transition to technology-infused classrooms has failed to significantly impact student learning in the United States and in most systems. The digital world surrounds students outside of school and, to an increasing degree, inside of school, but they have not become better learners. For example, the Organisation for Economic Co-operation and Development (OCED, 2015) report finds no correlation between the amount of money spent on technology by countries and their success in student learning. Deep learning, by contrast, does make a difference because it alters pedagogy in ways that engage students in their own learning and links this to global competencies like the six Cs: character, citizenship, collaboration, communication, creativity, and critical thinking (New Pedagogies for Deep Learning, n.d.). As we show in this book, strong new learning partnerships between students, teachers, and families must shape and propel deep learning for students to become better learners today, and for the future.

We aim to show how learning can be radically different and fulfilling for a majority of students and educators—*stratospheric* is the word we like to use—and how this kind of successful technology-based change can be implemented on a whole-system basis (districtwide and schoolwide). We also hope to pave the way for states, provinces, and countries to move in this direction.

This chapter discusses the siren call of technology and its limited impact on educational progress. We write about the importance of building change knowledge and avoiding digital dabbling to generate a growth culture that uses technology and professional capital together to build unstoppable momentum.

The Siren Call of Technology

Many states and districts across the United States have fallen for the beckoning sirens of digital nirvana. Just as the sirens of Greek mythology, with their beautiful voices, lured sailors to crash on the reefs, the siren songs of technology have lured educators and students into a sea of confusion and wreckage. One such example involves the Los Angeles Unified School District, which entered a $1 billon contract with Apple and Pearson to supply curricula-loaded iPads to teachers and students only to abort the contract within one year because it didn't fully understand how to implement the technology (Blume, 2014). Eric Sheninger and Thomas C. Murray (2017) document countless other examples of false starts.

These kinds of problems arise when educators use technology as the starting point. Technology appears concrete and sexy, and human beings tend to take the path of least resistance and go with the latest toys—a kind of *shiny object syndrome*. Even from a budget standpoint, one-shot computer purchases are appealing because the expenditure does not necessarily go in the base budget.

When schools buy or upgrade technology platforms, they often think they have moved into 21st century learning. But many have not developed the culture and environment that are equally necessary for student success in the 21st century. Now that the digital movement is fully underway, schools are generally adopting an *acquisition strategy*. They believe they are moving forward just by the act of buying machines. However, just as many golfers and tennis players have found, if their fundamentals are not sound, the latest equipment does not guarantee improvements in expertise and performance.

The state of technology use in many U.S. districts amounts to little more than digital dabbling. This is understandable given the explosive nature of digital innovations and plethora of options, but digital dabbling, as we write about in more detail later in this chapter, often represents a significant waste of resources and opportunities. Most school systems use technology superficially or wrongly because they are attracted to the quick fix of purchased modernity without realizing the fundamental foundation work that must underpin the effective use of digitally related solutions. Many districts put the focus on hardware when it should be on *heartware*, that is, on the human infrastructure rather than the technical infrastructure. Often school leaders look for a quick tick rather than the long lift that complex and systemic change requires. Getting it right is not easy. In this book, we outline the new thinking and actions that must underpin the use of technology in order to achieve the goal of improving learning for *all* students.

The problem is especially pressing because traditional schooling is increasingly boring as students go up the grade levels, with barely one-third of students engaged in their schoolwork by the time they reach grade 9 or 10 (Jenkins, 2013; Sheninger & Murray, 2017). This leaves teachers worse off as well, because teaching bored students is not fun. Every year, Pew Charitable Trusts (www.pewtrusts .org) releases a report on student attitudes about high school, and every year a stunning majority of students tell us they see no connection between their school experience and their future.

In *Stratosphere*, Fullan (2013) laments the lack of integration of three potentially powerful learning forces—(1) technology, (2) pedagogy, and (3) change knowledge. For a long time, educators tried to keep technology at arm's length, but eventually there was no choice—digital technology is relentless and ubiquitous. But it's not sufficiently integrated. When technology deployments are not integrated with sound pedagogy and a wealth of change knowledge, its benefits are severely limited.

Limited Impact

It comes as no surprise that our most comprehensive educational researchers repeatedly find that technology has little impact on student engagement and learning. In *Visible Learning for Teachers*, John Hattie (2012) analyzes approximately nine hundred meta-research studies of instructional practices, calculates the effect sizes of more than two hundred teaching practices, and consistently finds that technology has an effect size of 0.15 (impact effects of 0.40 and above are significant). And Stanford University researcher Larry Cuban (2013) shows that the impact of technology on classroom practice has been insignificant since the 1970s.

Although the digital explosion is far more powerful than anything we have ever seen in education, Alan November (2012) reminds us that computers don't make people smarter, just as electric typewriters didn't make people smarter. Having access to all the information in the world does not make us better problem solvers. Technology per se does not create learning, and technology in and of itself is not the solution. A saying often attributed to Grady Booch, chief scientist in software engineering at IBM Research, goes, "A fool with a tool is still a fool." In short, technology as solution puts the cart before the horse. Pedagogy and culture are the foundations, as we show in the rest of this book.

To express our theory of action up front, we incorporate student engagement and learning impact, and the causal pathways to such impact, inside our model. We do this not for accountability reasons (although it serves that purpose), but rather because if you do not know your impact or how to get there, you will inevitably remain at the surface level. Many early large-scale deployments of laptops and efforts to transform the culture of learning and teaching showed exuberance and promising expectations, but fell flat over time.

Henrico County Public Schools in Virginia, for example, launched the first major districtwide one-to-one laptop program in 2000. The district gave every middle and high school student a laptop (twenty-six thousand in total) and implemented wireless connectivity in all schools. Visitors from all over the United States made their way to Richmond to see what this digital revolution looked like. The National School Boards Association even hailed it as a success (Sellers, 2002).

The state of Maine followed in 2001, deploying laptops to all middle school students in the state. Despite implementation challenges and logistical barriers, most observers saw great promise and opportunity in this bold initiative (Gravelle, 2003). Dozens of individual U.S. schools and a few districts launched similar programs.

Despite numerous efforts like these, we don't know of any districtwide digital programs that have altered teaching and learning or produced true accountability indicators of success. This is not to insinuate that none of these programs have experienced success, but rather that even in the most committed situations, with full digital coverage, the measurable learning impact has been small. Henrico was lauded for the bold initial effort, but change in leadership resulted in a systemic backing off from the implementation with inconsistent and spotty use. This is an important lesson that a lack of coherent direction will kill most, if not all, efforts for district transformation.

Although there are examples of carefully planned and orchestrated technology, very few have paid attention to corresponding pedagogy and culture that are essential for success in learning and student achievement. Technology becomes an end to itself and overlooks the real drivers—engaging pedagogy and collaborative cultures that build change knowledge and efficacy of results.

Time and again, districts are looking for solutions in the wrong places. When pressure mounts for results, as it has increasingly since No Child Left Behind (NCLB; 2001–2002) in the United States, and when shiny objects grab the attention of leaders and sponsors, it is inevitable that people want tangible solutions. Even though the Every Student Succeeds Act (ESSA; 2015–2016) replaced NCLB in the United States, there is no indication that the system has learned its lesson. It is becoming very clear that the pedagogical transformation of deep learning requires a cultural foundation that provides for the systemic coherence that is necessary for this work.

In sum, despite the millions of dollars invested and the hundreds of schools embracing digital resources and new instructional practices, there is an absence of models that indicate long-term, improved student outcomes and significant evolution of teaching and learning practices. This book aims to provide such a model of successful transformational change.

Change Knowledge

To say that technology has a limited impact on learning is not to deny the power of technology. Technology works when partnered with a professional capital framework, pedagogy, and change knowledge. Pedagogy is at the heart of learning, and change knowledge deals with motivating and supporting large numbers of people throughout the change process. The solution must focus on the whole system—all schools in a jurisdiction, sound pedagogy, and a link to measurable outcomes. Cutting across these three dimensions is change knowledge. *Change knowledge* involves what educators need to know to navigate the change process effectively, as a participant or leader, leading to greater ownership and impact.

According to David Cote, the former CEO of Honeywell, the most important thing about leadership is to be right at the end of the meeting, not the beginning (Solomon, 2014). To be right at the end of the meeting means that the group has processed complex ideas—developing clarity, capacity, and commitment in relation to an important goal and figuring out the best way to address that goal throughout the change process. An effective change process is one that shapes and reshapes good ideas as it builds capacity and ownership. There are two components to the definition. First, there is the quality of the idea. Second, there is the quality of the process to build new capacities. Change leadership involves bringing these two aspects together. For educators, integrating good ideas with capacity building is at the heart of our coherence framework solution to system change (Fullan & Quinn, 2016). We have found that when this is done well, the change process becomes voluntary but inevitable, as you will see in the following chapters. For example, although people in MGSD never imposed deep change, it occurred, and virtually everyone in the district came to embrace it.

In a good change process, people value each other and the ideas because they have had a say in the matter and because the ideas work. When the change process fails to attract buy-in from its stakeholders, it is often because the process involves digital dabbling.

Digital Dabbling

Unfortunately, superficial change in technology use, where the devices appear but teaching doesn't change, seems to be the norm. We have seen district after district purchase tablets using a plan that boiled down to just putting some stuff out there and seeing what happens. In these cases, usually not much happens, or the lack of deep conviction for sustained learning from educators generates messy and incoherent results. We believe educators and districts are increasingly realizing that technology adoption alone is not working. They are worried about the limited impact and lack of results we discussed earlier in this chapter and are seeking new approaches to address these problems. Our goal is to help provide a road map to enable the transition from technology's false promise to establishing learning as the foundation. Next, we summarize the babble problem and, in subsequent chapters, move toward a systematic solution.

Dabble Babble

Stories abound of digital initiatives in schools that soon fade. Doing the "laptop thing" achieves little, except to tell students that schools are not the places to learn. Students know that mere knowledge acquisition is not learning, and that they can get the content answer to almost any problem with the push of a button. Too much focus on using technology to quickly get easy answers all but guarantees a superficial or inconsequential outcome and manifests among students and staff as a lack of long-term interest in real change.

You can often immediately tell the difference between a well-planned and implemented technology rollout from one that involves dabbling. We have heard these comments from education leaders indicating the dabbling problem.

- "We are focused on a smooth deployment."
- "Choosing the right device is first and foremost."
- "We have completed our plan."
- "We are rolling out carts and can't wait to see the change."
- "We are focusing on innovation and fun."
- "We don't send the laptops home."
- "This will make life easier for teachers."
- "We have a six-year rollout plan."
- "We are rolling out to everyone in the first year."
- "We are debating bring your own device (BYOD) and other alternatives."

These sorts of statements are indicative of reliance on jargon in place of a crafted implementation plan. For example, "We are focusing on innovation and fun" provides no concrete details for how a device rollout will benefit teachers or students. It's a litany of nonspecific platitudes rather than a plan of concrete processes to achieve results. If your district often communicates in this manner, it is time to stop and consider how to address the dabble deficits in your technology rollout plan.

Dabble Deficits

Devices are essential to the change process but only one part of a long journey, and the other parts are often overlooked. Districts often buy a little bit of this software and a little bit of that, hoping that something good will happen. But dabbling—without commitment to and focus on pedagogy and the culture; without investing in a sense of team and family in the classrooms, schools, and district; and without attention to the following common deficits—will guarantee limited progress.

- Lack of short- and long-term learning goals
- Lack of alignment and coherence
- Leader turnover or lack of leadership
- Goal changes midstream
- Acceptance of mediocrity
- Politics and institutional resistance
- Financial and resource issues
- Lack of human capital
- Lack of social capital
- Lack of decisional capital
- State and federal mixed messages about priorities
- A poor or weak culture
- Lack of collective will
- Lack of momentum
- Lack of communication with stakeholders
- Lack of professional development for teachers and administrators

From the beginning, it is important to realize that, even with the most carefully laid plans, the change process is complex and messy;

people will make mistakes. But a stream of unconnected initiatives, avoidance of problems, and fear of the unknown are hugely detrimental to any efforts to innovate and change.

A lack of coherent information and dialogue with students, teachers, administrators, school board members, parents, and community members usually means that bad information infects the culture. Issuing directives or presenting plans without formative dialogue leaves individuals and teams with a sense of helplessness when working through challenges. Worst of all, when bumps and turbulence occur, avoiding the work or becoming cynical has a hugely negative impact. It doesn't have to be this way. It is time to put culture and technology together.

Culture and Technology Together

Digital content is loaded with great new functionality that can potentially benefit students, teachers, and administrators. Many times, however, schools build the professional development around the use of the technology without allowing for personal and collective growth. For example, supporting principals to grow in leading change, as well as inculcating teachers in leadership, are essential and vital to digital innovation work. The real digital energy comes from the opportunities to connect learners to their work and constructing collaborative projects that mirror real-world work.

Neglecting the important work of building human, social, and decisional capital is at the root of widespread mediocrity and dismal progress in many digital initiatives, as Andy Hargreaves and Michael Fullan (2012) so thoroughly document. The working conditions that support the new pedagogical dynamic we see on the horizon require a level of systemic alignment and leadership continuity that constantly lifts and reflects on classroom work. In the rest of the book we show how one district—Mooresville Graded School District in North Carolina—got it right, and how other districts are taking up the lessons it learned. There is nothing mysterious about implementing the strategies and processes leading to success. It requires a strong sense of moral purpose to serve all students, but more than that, it involves a clear and persistent approach to change and mobilize a collective culture devoted to adult and student learning linked to measurable impact.

DEEP LEARNING

Achieving stratospheric success in implementing technology in education is like an iceberg. The technology is clearly visible, but below the surface is something much larger that really counts. This something is where we find *deep learning*, a melding of skills and attributes that range from critical thinking and problem solving to citizenship and creativity. The deep learning process also includes the necessary pedagogy transformation to develop these new competencies. In this chapter, we outline the effective deep learning programs in the Mooresville Graded School District, where Mark A. Edwards was superintendent.

Andy Hargreaves and his colleagues (2014) describe the lens through which to view a district's success in *Uplifting Leadership*— successful systems learn from, but never imitate, other effective organizations. We explore how you can establish your district's own cultural transformation, the driving factors that cata-lyze innovation, and the people and groups working to extend con-nections that advance knowledge across both district and country lines. We conclude with a threefold model for professional capital that sets up much of the rest of this book.

Mooresville Graded School District

Both *Every Child, Every Day* (Edwards, 2014) and *Thank You for Your Leadership* (Edwards, 2016) outline the MGSD transfor-mational process. This district has approximately 6,200 students in seven schools and a technical education center affiliated with the high school. Free and reduced lunch eligibility has increased to about 40 percent of the student population since the economic downturn in 2008. The student population is 72 percent Caucasian, 18 percent African American, and 8 percent Hispanic.

In 2007, MGSD embarked on a digital conversion of all schools—from a paper-based to a digital world in which every student and teacher has access to a computer device and to anywhere, anytime Internet. This is the tip of the iceberg. In 2015, MGSD ranked 99th of 115 North Carolina districts in per-pupil funding from all sources (local, state, and federal). Despite this disadvantage, the district's graduation rate jumped to 93 percent (second in the state) and its academic performance to 89 percent (third in the state) in 2011. The district has maintained this improvement. In fact, all academic and attendance performance indicators have increased steadily since 2008. For example, according to data from the North Carolina Department of Public Instruction (n.d.a, n.d.b), academic district performance increased from 73 to 90 percent between 2007 and 2015; graduation rates from 70 percent in 2007 to 90 percent in 2015; and so on. Table 2.1 and figure 2.1 illustrate the district's stark improvement.

Table 2.1: North Carolina District Achievement, 2014–2015

Rank	District	2014–2015 Proficiency
1	Chapel Hill-Carrboro	77 percent
2	Union	72 percent
	Polk	72 percent
3	Mooresville Graded	71 percent

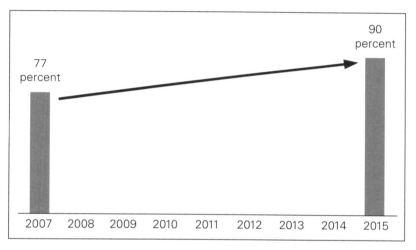

Figure 2.1: Four-year cohort graduation rate at MGSD.

Based on the MGSD experience, we developed a set of guidelines to help districts move rapidly and soundly to stratospheric deep learning performance on a systemwide basis. The following eight guidelines reflect the elements of whole-system change (Fullan, 2010).

1. Moral imperative (high expectations for all students)
2. Culture of caring (caring for all with a push for efficacy)
3. Digital resources and infrastructure (support, ubiquity of access)
4. Evolutional capacity building (individual and team)
5. Instructional transformation (new pedagogy for student and teacher engagement)

6. Daily date with data (building an evidence-based culture)

7. Resource alignment (establishing priorities and repurposing resources accordingly)

8. All-in collaboration (everyone counts and is implicated)

These elements gain their power through their interaction with each other. A cookbook recipe or an organizational change model is impossible because the dynamics are often subtle and many issues are peculiar to a given culture. However, schools can do a much better job of getting at the key factors and their interactions. The following key factors played a major role in the MGSD results.

- Coalescing leaders at all levels around a shared vision (developing coordinated leadership at the school and district levels)

- Establishing leadership for high performance (adjusting to the push and pull of change)

- Creating a culture for collaborative work (with focus and specificity)

- Developing an evidenced-based culture (availability, transparency, precision of data for action)

- Establishing leadership development for all (informal and formal processes for leading and learning at all levels)

- Managing the tough stuff within a caring climate (being accountable internally at the district level and externally at the state or province level)

These six factors in concert framed the shift in culture at MGSD. Constant reflective dialogue in which staff routinely asked questions like "How is the work going?" and "What are we learning?" provided everyone with a shared feeling and purpose of their role in authoring the transformation story. By applying these guidelines and key factors in a way that addresses your district's unique needs, you can begin the process of establishing a cultural transformation that achieves measurable results for your entire student body.

Cultural Transformation

A successful change process involves developing a culture where everyone models and expects visibility; practice and results are transparent; action is precise; problem solving is innovative, but disciplined; and everyone is engaged each day. At MGSD, *everyone* means students, parents, janitors, clerical staff, teachers, and administrators at *all* levels. One effective way of developing and reinforcing this kind of culture is to expect that everyone becomes a teacher for everyone else, inside and outside of the district. This is a win-win proposition that helps everyone get better as they develop "a shared understanding about the nature of the work" (Fullan & Quinn, 2016, p. 2).

To create this shared understanding, schools must combine a compelling vision with purposeful day-to-day interaction to help people learn to *talk the walk.* When people can easily explain in clear terms what they are doing and with what results, it is clear to everyone that the work is genuine. When many people can consistently do this, they influence each other's actions, skills, and commitment. As the culture becomes stronger in shared understanding, two other phenomena occur: coherence and the strengthening of relationships. After we establish these concepts we'll examine why this learn-by-doing philosophy worked for the MGSD.

Shared Coherence

Coherence is the bugbear of organizations and especially school systems. Coherence concerns the degree to which people at the school and district levels have a common sense of the district's core priorities and how to achieve them. Education leaders usually try to achieve coherence through greater alignment of goals, resources, training, and so on, but structural alignment on paper does not produce subjective coherence in the minds of organization members. So, we need to replace the concept of alignment with the more powerful concept of coherence or, more precisely, *shared coherence.* There are no shortcuts to shared coherence. To achieve it, schools must constantly make a relentless effort to implement the guidelines and factors listed in the Mooresville Graded School District section of this chapter (page 18). Alignment is important but it is not enough. Everyone involved must share a deep conviction about their work. They must not just go along for the ride, but commit to getting to some new place—a place of cultural coherency.

Relationship Building

In addition to shared coherence, the other phenomenon that develops is deep relationships with the community, businesses, and other districts. MGSD invests in relationship building by welcoming numerous visitors every year and learning from them. Relationships at MGSD are a constant source of energy and vitality to every area of work. Schools and districts thank and recognize custodians and cafeteria staff. They show respect and appreciation for bus drivers and maintenance staff. Veteran teachers embrace and lift new teachers. Over the years, a prevailing sense of being in it together becomes a daily cultural dynamic that everyone holds onto. It may seem cliché but it really is about a sense of belonging and family that holds enormous value.

As the district developed its own internal high-level capacity, staff members began engaging in an increasing number of external consultancies, training others in districts across the United States. Due in part to these relationships, other schools and districts have recruited and promoted several MGSD leaders as superintendents, assistant superintendents, principals, and so on. These changes create vacancies at MGSD, but the district's culture ensures that new leaders consistently step up, continuing and advancing the district's work. Put another way, effective districts are continually developing new leadership, which enables them to replenish internal leadership when required as well as extend the network of influence and learning across the country.

Learning by Doing

We learn by doing and by teaching others. The skills needed to ensure shared coherence and to build relationships are not there on day one. These skills include developing specific instructional methods, assessing their impact on learning, and identifying and spreading effective practices throughout the district. Leading students in a collaborative or project-based environment requires complex situational and leadership skills that take time and commitment to develop. It's like being a roaming orchestra director.

We all must learn and grow to be helpful to others, but once a critical mass of people becomes skillful, people learn deeply from each other, and the ongoing learning builds into the culture. When scores of people occupy these lead-learner roles, the learning becomes geometric and sustainable. Very specific human and social factors such as these are at the root of successful change—the kind that cannot be bought but must be cultivated.

We believe that the time is right for deep learning (such as that achieved at MGSD) to expand on a wider scale—for stratospheric takeoff in many other jurisdictions. Conditions and opportunity are coming together for schools, districts, students, and teachers all over the United States and the world, where a synergistic effect is propelling innovation advancements. Although it takes time for these actions to result in measurable results (the lag effect), we are now seeing the lights of innovation and stratospheric teaching and learning pop up in many places. You will read firsthand accounts from leaders in several of these places in chapter 7.

Driving Factors

Several driving factors serve as innovation catalysts, giving a broad lift to districts surging into digital conversions, with exciting implications for how teachers teach and how students learn. Driving this movement is the grassroots leadership of superintendents, principals, teachers, and students who want to leverage new pedagogies, collaborative cultures, and rich digital resources into new and deeper learning.

We are seeing the long-awaited integration of the three forces we mentioned previously—technology, pedagogy, and change knowledge. Purposeful leadership supports this array of converging forces with the following driving factors.

Hardware

Technology, as we have argued, is not a driver of pedagogical change, but it can and should be an accelerator of learning. Accordingly, it is critical to choose hardware for your district that best supports its learning goals. Hardware options for modern classrooms are abundant, and price points continue to decline. Many laptops, tablets, and other devices now address classroom and student work as part of the product design. More durable machines are now available, with form and function designed for student project work, self-directed learning, and collaboration. Many districts have figured out a financial formula to fund hardware purchases, such as using a leasing program to spread costs over several years. For example, the MGSD model focused on repurposing existing funding rather than seeking new funding. This included purchasing digital content instead of books rather than in addition to them.

Wireless Infrastructure

Wireless infrastructure has evolved along a parallel path with hardware, with advancements in speed, dependability, and accessibility for schools and students. When former U.S. President Barack Obama visited MGSD in June 2013 to announce the Federal Trade Commission ConnectED initiative (U.S. Department of Education, n.d.), he brought great news to many schools across the country. ConnectED reconfigures E-Rate funding to increase the number of U.S. schools with broadband access—a clear signal to educators that it is time to get the digital game on. In addition to schools, *community conduits* are available in public libraries, churches, recreation centers, laundromats, ball fields, and buses to give students greater access to the Internet to support their learning. Engaging with local broadband providers through community collaboration with elected officials, chambers of commerce, economic development groups, as well as service organizations can help ensure their services reach more families.

Digital Content

Hardware and wireless infrastructures are merely platforms to deliver learning experiences. You still need to load them with access to content. Fortunately, digital content is rapidly improving in quality, functionality, affordability, and variety, bringing richness to student and teacher work and rendering traditional textbooks not only obsolete but also poor investments. Textbooks are more expensive to purchase in the first place, are less flexible to update, contain less information, and become obsolete more quickly. By contrast, search engines and links to related content, movies, photos, and media sources have added new learning support that is changing the work of students and teachers forever.

In this stratospheric advancement, we see students engineering their own learning, as well as teachers who design personalized instruction and collaborative networks that produce meaningful results. For example, MGSD students have intimate knowledge about their learning through real-time information they receive every day. They are cognizant of their progress, and they can build their work plans by using personalized information and feedback to guide their focus. Embedded assessment engines give students and teachers real-time learning data for personal and classroom use.

The integration of multimedia, design graphics, and presentation software into student work has brought a giant leap forward in quality. Project RED (One-to-One Institute, n.d.) provided clear illumination of the exciting evolving digital content offerings that match student learning to what students are seeing in social media, entertainment, and just about every aspect of their life. Students are mapping out their work and building personalized learning trajectories. They are excited and engaged about using real-world resources as they see their progress and begin to own their learning.

Collaborative Communities

Collaborative communities represent a dramatic new dynamic in the digital classroom for students and teachers, with vibrant new opportunities for connected learning. Sheninger and Murray (2017) identify eight themes that make these new learning communities much more effective (themes one will readily find at MGSD): (1) creating a culture of innovation, (2) redesigning the learning experience, (3) ensuring a return on instruction, (4) designing learner-centered spaces, (5) making professional learning personal, (6) leveraging technology, (7) collaborating and engaging with the community, and (8) leading the charge.

In MGSD, teachers participate in collaborative knowledge advancement through dozens of online learning and sharing communities. They have found a powerful new way to learn, grow, and build collegial relationships by connecting their work with national and international pioneers in the new stratosphere. And for students, learning how to work with other communities lets them see their work in relation to the work of others—a great preparation for life.

Projects and Presentations

Individual and team projects and presentations are integral design elements of students' and teachers' daily work. At MGSD, students are constantly involved in constructing collaborative projects to deepen their learning and to share what they have learned and how they learned it. In one example, a team of Mooresville High School students entered an invention competition and developed what they called "a new drag kit for trucks" that would cut down on wind resistance and increase fuel efficiency. The students didn't win the competition (they took third place), but they all grew from the experience. In this way, students are becoming adroit at building digital products that include advanced research and artistic presentations that greatly enhance their communication and social skills, adding a fluid and dynamic element to teaching and learning that provides a daily dose of freshness and fun.

New Leadership Skills

Nothing is more important in the change process than leadership and leadership design, which turbocharge transformational change. We are now seeing some superintendents push leadership responsibilities out to every school and classroom. Peer mentoring and team mentoring by grade level and establishing department chairs constitute a way to bring formative leadership nurturance to daily work. Media specialist and tech and teaching coaches add a distributed cultural energy to the workplace by connecting peers to grow together. These teacher leaders and coaches are becoming ubiquitous and shaping the culture and work disposition of students and peers. Student leaders are evolving from opportunity and necessity. We see these new leadership opportunities throughout MGSD, and in chapter 7 we provide vignettes from six other districts that have learned from Mooresville as they developed their own versions.

With the huge amount of information now available to students and teachers, spontaneous student leadership is an integral part of the dialogue around class assignments and presentations. MGSD deliberately cultivates and develops student leadership and agency in their own learning, all of which the new district culture and corresponding leveraging of digital power enable. We routinely see students at MGSD engaging in research and then reporting back to the class what they learned. Student voice is an integral part of the instructional flow and is foundational to the new pedagogy of deep learning. Likewise, the development of central office staff, principals, and assistant principals to lead in this new dynamic environment, as well as to develop a new school culture, is a growing priority for most school districts, and is certainly exemplified at MGSD.

Connections to Advance Knowledge

Districts of every size (including several very large districts) are engaging in digital immersion, but it is not at all clear how this work is grounded in changes in pedagogy, and accompanied by the kind of change leadership required for the learning transformation we've seen at MGSD. We wrote this book to convey to others how pervasive and fundamental the stratospheric change must be to be successful.

As momentum builds at the district level, several educational organizations are helping to advance the knowledge base and connect leaders with best practices to turbocharge innovation and digital conversion. The School Superintendents Association (or AASA) initiated a digital consortium of over thirty districts leading innovation excellence (www.aasa.org/DigitalConsortium.aspx), and Executive Director Daniel A. Domenech is focusing on advancing school and district leadership. The Consortium for School Networking (CoSN; www.cosn.org), under the leadership of CEO Keith R. Krueger, is growing new state affiliates and providing regional professional development for district leaders all over the United States. The National School Boards Association (https://nsba.org), with Director of Education Technology Ann Flynn leading the charge, continues to encourage digital innovation efforts. Finally, the League of Innovative Schools (http://digitalpromise.org/initiative/league-of -innovative-schools) is highlighting district innovation and collaborative networks to advance the work of school transformation.

These efforts don't exist just within U.S. borders. As one would expect, this is a worldwide phenomenon as countries try to develop global competencies in their schools that are essential for the present and the future. New Pedagogies for Deep Learning (www.npdl .global) is one such initiative across seven countries: (1) Australia,

(2) Canada, (3) Finland, (4) the Netherlands, (5) New Zealand, (6) Uruguay, and (7) the United States (Fullan, Quinn, & McEachen, in press). This global partnership is made up of seven clusters involving twelve hundred schools. Each cluster consists of sets of schools from specific districts or municipalities. The clusters develop and learn from each other within and across countries. In short, MGSD is part of a worldwide phenomenon.

chapter three

PROFESSIONAL CAPITAL OF TEACHERS: SOCIAL CAPITAL

Despite the number of districts embarking on digital initiatives, as we have said, very few have developed a whole-system solution with integrated technology, pedagogy, and change knowledge. The framework that Hargreaves & Fullan (2012) developed on *the professional capital of teachers* provides a useful organizer that we can use to capture the change in culture at MGSD. The capital concept refers to a resource that becomes more and more enriched as it circulates. Professional capital is such a resource and consists of three components that are fueled by a strong, relentless moral purpose and uplifting leadership (see figure 3.1, page 32). We believe that this model captures the strategy, culture, and success at MGSD, and we use it as the organizer for this chapter (social capital), as well as chapters 4 (human capital) and 5 (decisional capital).

Figure 3.1: Core components of professional capital.

Surrounding the capitals in figure 3.1 are the concepts of moral imperative and uplifting leadership. Moral imperatives, such as targeting success for all students, appear in almost every district's mission and vision statements. We believe that unless there is a strong strategy to accomplish one's moral imperative it remains an empty slogan. Thus, MGSD's relentless moral imperative is one that becomes embedded in its culture, through the development of professional capital. Similarly, leadership must be uplifting in that it permeates and inspires all individuals and groups in the district. It is this leadership that makes the moral imperative a day-to-day reality. A strong element of MGSD's success involves the widespread cultivation of leadership in all quarters of the district, along with careful attention to developing a cadre of ongoing and future leaders.

Of the three capitals—human, social, and decisional—we start in this chapter with social capital because it strongly supports both human capital and decisional capital. We cover this concept in detail and then show how you can continue to build it through shared leadership and talking the walk.

Social Capital

Social capital pertains primarily to the quality of the group while also developing individuals (human capital) and fostering evidence-based decision making (decisional capital). Social capital consists of collaborative cultures committed to the student achievement agenda and effective at accomplishing it. Note that collaboration itself is not the point; people can collaborate to do superficial things or even to do the wrong thing. It is only when teams focus specifically on best practices that help each and every child learn—when they examine what they are doing, and learn how to do it better and better—and when it permeates the culture of the district that we can claim that effective social capital is at work.

Business professor Carrie R. Leana, based at the University of Pittsburgh, who has studied social capital for more than a decade, typically uses these three measurements in schools.

1. Teacher qualifications (human capital)

2. Teacher responses to questions such as, "To what extent do you and other teachers work together to improve the learning of all students in the school?" (social capital)

3. Progress in mathematics achievement over the course of a year (Leana, 2011)

Leana (2011) finds that while individual teachers with high human capital get results, by far the greatest overall mathematics results occur in schools with high social capital. The main reason that this occurs is that they focus together on what works, learning and consolidating as they go. They spread good ideas across classrooms, and schools in the district. The cumulative effect is powerful.

Social capital also has a spillover effect on teachers who are struggling. Leana found that teachers with lower human capital in high social capital schools also tend to improve in mathematics achievement. In other words, group strengths make up for individual shortcomings. Similarly, Hattie (2015), a leading researcher on the impact of specific teaching practices on student achievement, finds that collaborative expertise has the greatest positive impact on students.

Social capital is even more critical when schools are innovating, because people must learn new things rapidly. When people work together on new solutions, innovation happens—and at a much faster pace. In short, the highest leverage for any district involves developing purposeful, focused, skilled collaboration within and between schools.

In our work, we find time and again that principals who focus on developing the group have the greatest impact (Fullan, 2014; Fullan & Quinn, 2016) and that collaborative group cultures lead to greater shared coherence. The group, in this case, includes everyone from teachers and administrators to all support personnel. Our rule of thumb is *Use the group to change the group.*

In the MGSD, leaders combined moral purpose and collaboration to develop a caring group culture that includes several main elements (Edwards, 2014).

- Commitment to every individual
- Committed leadership at all levels
- Communication of caring expectations
- Ongoing appreciation of individuals and teams
- Professional development on how to care for students
- Involvement of every employee in the mission of learning
- Management of negative elements
- Participatory decision making at all levels
- Laughter and fun as cultural norms

Over a four-year period (2008–2012), MGSD saw and felt an instructional boom or uplift from the interplay of these factors. As Edwards experienced firsthand, attendance went up, suspensions went down, and student achievement increased in multiple areas. Students were engaged and became forces for change themselves, providing feedback to teachers and helping each other. This collaboration served the goal of instructional transformation and helped students move from boredom to excitement. This success didn't go unnoticed, as guests frequently visited to see what students and teachers were doing in classrooms. The *New York Times* (Schwarz, 2012) and Fox News (Williams, 2012) both reported on the success and agreed that there was something special happening at MGSD.

MGSD uses the phrase *all in* to indicate the systemwide collaboration that led to the district's synergy and momentum (Edwards, 2014). Everyone was drawn into the collective effort—students, support staff, parents, maintenance workers, bus drivers, and janitors, as well as educators. As MGSD illustrates, it is difficult for people to resist the pull of working with others or refuse to join in a collective effort. Most go along and then find that the common goal invigorates them.

Every summer, MGSD holds a Summer Connection, a professional development institute that models collaboration and social capital (Mooresville Graded School District, n.d.). The institute is optional, but 90 percent of staff participate each year. The agenda varies depending on the focus, but the collaborative social element is always there, helping to build the social capital reinforced throughout the school year via professional development. A glance at the 2016 summer institute agenda gives an idea of the detailed and wide-ranging skills addressed: instructional leadership; tools to improve instruction and achievement; best practices sharing; leveraging parent partnerships to discuss data; addressing the performance gap; data-driven goal setting; making global connections; student collaboration; and many others. These summer institutes serve as miniuniversities for all staff and hundreds of others from other districts. For the MGSD staff, the ideas examined in the summer are linked to the implementation of school development plans.

Shared Leadership

As described in Edwards's 2016 book *Thank You for Your Leadership*, MGSD's leadership is a collective, social endeavor. It does not come from the top down, but from collaborative efforts at every level, with teachers working in teams to achieve common goals. In successful districts, we see time and again that leaders at all levels learn and lead in equal measure. (You can't lead if you are not learning.) Moreover, people learn from each other both laterally—from their peers—and vertically—from those above and those below them in the organization (Fullan & Quinn, 2016). When we see such leading and learning in everyday practice, as is the case in MGSD, it inevitably leads to ongoing student performance improvement. The focus is on building the cultural conditions for shared leadership, because when people work collaboratively to jointly develop skills in a digital conversion initiative, the force of that effort meets the lift from teachers and students that grow and achieve success over time.

With effective shared leadership in place, districts can focus on making sure that everyone talks the walk. For example, grade-level and department chairs at MGSD evolved as true instructional leaders who analyzed their efforts, studied data, and designed formative strategies to address teacher peers or student needs. At quarterly data meetings, teachers led the discussion of data analysis and constructed the plans to utilize the data.

Talking the Walk

In all successful systems, people individually and collectively *talk the walk*. This means that their work is transparent, precise, and linked to results, so they can pinpoint what is happening, why it is working, and what needs improvement—a coherent and subjective phenomenon (Fullan & Quinn, 2016).

One of the great benefits of strong social capital is that people talk the walk together, sharing a deep understanding about the nature of their work through ongoing and purposeful collaboration. Over time, shared skills and shared convictions arise, including the following:

- Every child means *every child*—no exceptions.
- Confidence in every child takes work and does not come easily.
- Working at working together, however difficult, translates into progress for children.
- Everyone needs to demonstrate a voracious appetite for learning.
- Working through disagreements and turbulence is essential for the good of students.
- Every day is unlike any other day, and we must live up to the opportunity.

Talking the walk means that no one just takes a single leader's word for it. It means that in every nook and cranny of the district, people can provide specifics about what they are doing and the details are consistent across individuals, without them having to check with each other. When people can talk the walk, they are conscious of what they are doing and why. When groups talk the walk, they are acting in mutually influential ways. When scores of system members consistently display and articulate goals and practices, groups are talking the walk and building continuous progress (Edwards, 2014, 2016). This action not only builds your social capital but also extends to your acquisition of human capital.

Social and Human Capital Interrelations

Social capital is the center of gravity for deep change, but only when it is thorough and incorporates human capital. For example, if teachers with less than highly effective practices share with each other, social capital may result, but not the kind of social capital that contributes to deep change. It is only when individuals and the group work to make each other stronger that social capital thrives. Social and human capital must go together, and if they do not, both are weakened.

Social capital in the absence of equal investment in human capital is superficial. And focusing on human capital while ignoring the culture of the group is a recipe for frustration. It will gradually erode staff quality because good people will not want to stay in ineffective cultures. The two are symbiotic and feed into each other. In sum, a powerful force in the MGSD involves investment in the staff's deep and specific knowledge and skills, especially those that focus on collaborative work tied to school achievement results. We can now turn to examine how the district fuels social capital with its focus on ubiquitous human capital development.

chapter four

PROFESSIONAL CAPITAL OF TEACHERS: HUMAN CAPITAL

Policymakers often start and end with *human capital*, the sum of the staff's individual knowledge and skill, because it seems obvious that high-quality leaders should focus on developing high-quality staff. However, the truth is that individuals rarely change cultures by themselves. In other words, human capital strategies by themselves tend to be wasted unless they are tied to team or collaborative development. As Hargreaves and Fullan (2012) put it:

> If you concentrate your efforts on increasing individual talent, you will have a devil of a time producing social capital. There is just no mechanism or motivation to bring all the talent together. The reverse is not true. High social capital does generate increased human capital. Individuals get confidence, learning and feedback from having the right kind of people and the right kinds of interactions and relationships around them. (p. 4)

It is sometimes necessary for leaders to take on a toxic culture alone, but this approach is generally ineffective in the long term and usually a recipe for leadership burnout. Bad or ineffective cultures tend to eat up good individuals faster than leaders can produce them. We focused on describing social capital first—the more complex goal of developing the group—but leaders must concentrate on both individual (human) and social capital from the start, while clearly communicating that cultural change is the first priority.

MGSD, for example, focused on developing collaborative cultures as a route to building human capital (Edwards, 2016). To kick-start building human capital, the initial focus was on securing leaders in key spots who could help develop individuals and the group. Once underway, the focus shifted to systematically developing everyone in the organization—from teachers and students to janitors and bus drivers. This approach is essential to secure deep and lasting change.

In this chapter, we discuss informal and formal leadership pathways, address accountability standards, and look at some methods for handling negaholics and other difficulties that may arise when you encounter pockets of resistance.

Leadership Pathways

Both informal and formal leadership pathways play a part at MGSD. Informal leadership development occurs when individuals are members of committees and groups that operate in a fashion where all members are learning to be more effective. Formal leadership pertains to designated roles, such as school principal, coach, department head, supervisor, head custodian, cafeteria manager, and so on. What is distinctive about learning organizations such as MGSD is that very large percentages of the organization learn about leadership because they are part of groups that are constantly learning and influencing one another.

Learning about leadership can come from a variety of sources, including the following.

- Department and grade-level chairs
- Digital curriculum committee members
- Teacher and principal selection committee members
- Teacher advisory committee members
- Calendar advisory members
- Summer institute staff
- Trainers of other districts
- Coaches, music directors, and sponsors of student organizations

Beyond these leadership roles, teachers encounter leadership opportunities daily. By taking advantage of opportunities like the following, teachers increase the value of their human capital.

- Reviewing and selecting new online content
- Monitoring content and processes for alignment with standards
- Troubleshooting content and assessment engines for students
- Sharing feedback with colleagues and service providers
- Using data to identify insights into student learning
- Mentoring new teachers

By making use of these opportunities, teachers create both an individual and a collective sense of learning and leading on an ongoing basis. As the ongoing culture takes root, it makes it clearer and easier to recruit new hires to buttress and deepen the culture.

MGSD systematically invests in the selection and orientation of all new employees, professional and classified. The district selects new hires based on the following qualities.

- Collaborative
- Collegially minded
- Effective
- Enthusiastic

- Growth oriented
- Ready to sweat

These qualities are in the service of the moral purpose and values that Mooresville espouses and can vary based on the unique nature of a district's culture. For example, what constitutes an effective new hire at MGSD is someone who deeply values or has a history of advancing student academic and personal development *and* is committed to working in a collaborative culture to maximize impact.

At an orientation each August, MGSD thoroughly introduces new staff members to the district and makes them aware of its culture and expectations. This orientation includes sending out an agenda for its New Employee Induction program, which looks similar to the one in figure 4.1. (The actual program also included the names of any speakers, in addition to their titles or organizations.)

MGSD New Employee Induction August 9–11, 2016 Day One Mooresville Intermediate School			
Agenda Item	**Topics Addressed**	**Length**	**Time**
Continental Breakfast Sign-In	Meet your new colleagues. Review agenda and objectives.	15 minutes	8:30–8:45 a.m.
MGSD Employee Introductions Director of Human Resources	MGSD leadership team New MGSD employees	15 minutes	8:45–9:00 a.m.
Welcome and Professional Charge	Joining the MGSD family All in Every child, every day	20 minutes	9:00–9:20 a.m.

Employee Assistance Program Life Systems Solutions	*A free district resource made available for you* Confidential and secure for you and your family May be referred or may use services voluntarily	5 minutes	9:20–9:25 a.m.
Curriculum and Instruction Assistant Principal, Mooresville Middle School Assistant Principal, Park View Elementary School	Elementary and intermediate instructional expectations Secondary instructional expectations The culture of our MGSD classrooms	45 minutes	9:30–10:15 a.m.
Morning break		10 minutes	10:15–10:25 a.m.
The Professional Educator and Use of Social Media Director of Public Information	Responsible use of social media as a professional educator Appropriate communication with students: "Dos and Don'ts"	60 minutes	10:30–11:30 a.m.
North Carolina Association of Educators Professional Teachers Organization President Vice President Beginning Teacher Leader	Introducing NCAE Becoming a member Benefits of NCAE membership	30 minutes	11:30 a.m.–12:00 p.m.

Figure 4.1: Agenda for day one of the MGSD New Employee Induction program.

continued

Lunch and informal sharing with MGSD school board members and principals		60 minutes	12:00–1:00 p.m.
MGSD Technology Training MGSD Instructional Technology Facilitators	Responsible Use Policy Technology tools and online resources LEARN	90 minutes	1:00–2:30 p.m.
MGSD Community Bus Tour*	Learn about Mooresville and visit its neighborhoods.	60 minutes	2:30–3:30 p.m.

*Afternoon bus tour of the MGSD schools and Mooresville community; you will board the bus at 2:30 p.m.

If you couple this orientation with the focus on teamwork and collaborative cultures you read about in chapter 3, you get a sense of the reciprocity between social and human capital. Strong individuals are hired and, in turn, become stronger as they learn from others doing the actual work of school improvement. Good people working with other good people produce even better people. It is an unstoppable combination!

It is this constant and specific attention to the details of social and human capital development that makes the difference in both the short and long run as the culture is embedded in the district's daily work. The many opportunities to learn at MGSD add up because they are built into the daily culture. These opportunities are much more powerful than formal professional development because not only do they integrate into the daily work but also have support from role models. Informal leadership opportunities to learn are hard to avoid and easy to access. The combined effect is to establish a culture where the work is learning and leading together. It is this combination that makes for effective performance (Fullan & Quinn, 2016). As Edwards put it with respect to MGSD, "Our teachers grow by working together on a constantly evolving ped-agogical framework in a student-centered, constructivist, and project-based classroom culture, with veteran and rookie teachers learning from each other."

In addition to the many ways to generate and develop human cap-ital from informal leadership practices, it is vital that you establish formal pathways, like the following, for developing staff.

• Doctoral and master's cohorts

• Leadership academies for assistant principals

• Teacher leader academies linked to each school

• Annual summer institutes

• Annual Summer Connection conferences

• Student and parent leadership programs

• Staff development for support staff and maintenance personnel

MGSD invests systematically in encouraging and enabling all staff to develop through formal leadership programs, regardless of how this might pay off for the district, although it usually does. On many occasions, when leadership positions opened, MGSD filled them with internal candidates in doctoral or master's cohorts that it identified as individuals ready and prepared for new leadership challenges.

One of the great motivators for employees is employer investment in their development—with courses and degrees that make staff more effective, more positioned for promotion, and more employable wherever they might go. Not everyone reacts positively to this idea. One possibly apocryphal story concerns the leader who complained that his organization was so good at developing its employees that other organizations hired them away. The response of course was, "Try not developing them and having them stay!" Indeed, there are concrete benefits to having well-developed staff move on.

In the case of the MGSD doctoral and master's cohorts, the district (sometimes with funds from the MGSD Foundation) pays $1,000 a year for tuition, and provides release time or courses held at convenient times. At MGSD, twenty-six of twenty-seven staff obtained their doctoral degrees between 2007–2015. Graduates included six principals and assistant principals, the director of exceptional children's services, and the director of human resources. In 2015, MGSD had a third master's cohort of nine graduates. Of these, five were promoted within the district and received several statewide honors, while four received promotions to other districts. All of this boosts the district's prestige, making it easier to attract and maintain even more talent. Districts that can develop talent need not fear losing individuals because the stronger its talent base, the more effective it becomes, even though its members become attractive sources of recruitment for other jurisdictions. In other words, being a hotbed of talent development is a sign of *internal* strength.

Teacher leaders conduct and focus on digitally based instruction at the annual summer institutes for teachers. More than three hundred teachers attended in the summer of 2012—including over 90 percent of the teachers in the district. The Summer Connection conferences attract districts from around the United States interested in digital conversion. Enrollment rose from two hundred fifty in 2010 to over four hundred in 2014.

Accountability

The center of gravity at MGSD is heavily weighted toward growth and responsibility, which fit perfectly with effective accountability. In *Coherence*, Michael Fullan and Joanne Quinn (2016) show that effective accountability is a combination of *internal accountability* (individuals and teams learning and reinforcing their own responsibility for performance) and *external accountability* (external standards, such as state assessments and graduation rates, addressing performance). Internal accountability is by far the more effective of the two accountabilities. Most organizations fail to achieve this. They become preoccupied with external requirements and fail to develop the more important internal responsibility—more important because sustaining your own success equips you to deal more effectively with external demands. At MGSD, one of the middle school department and content chairs, Allen Stevens, led a discussion about areas for improvement with these comments, "I know I can do better, and I know we can all do better. We have to work together and lift each other up. I plan on taking my game up a notch" (A. Stevens, personal communication, April 2015). MGSD invests carefully in helping individuals and groups increase their effectiveness, and has done so in a transparent and supportive way, only dealing with underperformance when other methods fail. In short, the district's internal accountability is very strong, which serves them well when they must relate to state standards.

As we discuss throughout this book, the three capitals (social, human, and decisional) combine to establish strong daily internal-to-external accountability that is highly effective, especially when compared with the usual state-driven external accountability. As schools establish a strong foundation of internal accountability, they can address most performance issues, freeing up leaders to address the remaining more manageable problems. Once schools invest in a results-oriented growth culture, that culture addresses accountability problems. This is never about a *let's be nice to everyone* way of working, because continuous progress on the moral imperative of helping all kids learn is a tough assignment. However, as a high-performance culture establishes a firm foundation of trust, most people embrace the fact that tough decisions must be made along the way.

The reality is that states impose increasingly large testing loads on districts. Whether this will change with the replacement of the No Child Left Behind Act (2001–2002) with the Every Student Succeeds Act (2015–2016) in the United States remains to be seen. Changes at the state level can be unpredictable, and there can be much ambiguity in external standards not under district control. MGSD handles this by relying on its internal strengths and focus, keeping teachers informed, and enlisting leaders to handle the pressure and figure out how best to manage the demands. The district's strong continuous-improvement track record means that staff are generally confident they can continue to identify what is best for students.

Negaholics and Other Problems

As discussed in *Every Child, Every Day* (Edwards, 2014), *negaholics* are team members who start out with a negative attitude. You can address negaholics using the following strategies:

- Treat negaholics with respect and affirm their good qualities.
- Affirm small steps.
- Provide examples of positive teacher work and its impact on student performance.
- Use data that show that teachers who embrace cultural and instructional transformation get better results.
- Get a witness to success; other formerly negaholic teachers that have changed.
- Evaluate negaholics on attitude, willingness to grow, teamwork, and student performance.
- Stand firm and expect most to become more effective. (Edwards, 2014, p. 35)

What has been especially effective in MGSD is that the vast majority of staff has grown on the job because the culture is so committed to learning and rewarding success. The so-called negaholics are very much in the minority, and this more or less reflects the adage that the exception proves the rule. Predominantly MGSD is a culture of growth for students and staff alike.

Given that education is a highly political and contentious domain, there are problems beyond managing negaholics that occur in the natural course of events. Such problems often occur in areas such as teacher performance, leader accountability, unwillingness to share information (or a silo mentality), politics, budget cuts, testing, and standards. Over the years, MGSD placed several teachers on improvement plans. Most responded and elevated their effort and productivity. A few did not improve and were eventually dismissed or counseled out.

Leaders are generally invested in getting it right. If this is not the case, however, leaders not serving their staff or students well are replaced. Their removal is necessary to maintain a trusting foundation with other staff members, the community, and students.

MGSD works hard to avoid the silo effect by promoting group collaboration and by acting when subgroups are not communicating or working at cross-purposes. With respect to its internal politics, MGSD works hard at prioritizing communication, seeking compromises, and keeping the focus on student learning. Similarly, the district handles state-imposed budget cuts openly with much of their underlying set of values of respect, growth, and appreciation intact.

The net effect of the ideas in the previous two chapters—a core of social capital combined with cultivation of talent from hiring onward—is to produce a system of crosscutting support backed up by high expectations, all of which leads to high performance. The number of problems becomes minimized and, with a growth mindset, the district addresses those problems that do occur. The collective development of capacity and examination of progress consolidate a culture of high performance. However, there is one more crucial element that must be incorporated: decisional capital.

chapter five

PROFESSIONAL CAPITAL OF TEACHERS: DECISIONAL CAPITAL

In our work, we have long recognized the importance of social and human capital. But over time, we came to realize that many collaborative efforts in schools are superficial or even wrongheaded, and that something else is at play. For example, in *Teachers Know Best*, the Boston Consulting Group (2014) found that while administrators frequently endorsed PLCs, only 29 percent of teachers felt the district met their professional development needs. When we look at the factors that strengthen other professions, we identify decisional capital as the missing link.

Experts in most fields have accumulated *decisional capital*—the gained wisdom and experience of weighing pros and cons, seeing patterns, making judgments, and so on. Consider this passage from Hargreaves and Fullan (2012):

> Making decisions in complex situations is what professionalism is all about. The pros do this all the time.

> They come to have competence, judgment, insight, inspiration, and the capacity for improvisation as they strive for exceptional performance. They do this when no one is looking, and they do it through and with their colleagues and the team. They exercise their judgments and decisions with collective responsibility, openness to feedback, and willing transparency. They are not afraid to make mistakes as long as they learn from them. They have pride in their work. They are respected by peers and by the public for knowing what they are doing. They strive to outdo themselves and each other in a spirit of making greater individual and collective contributions. (p. 5)

Unfortunately, this kind of expertise is not the teaching profession's strong suit. One reason is the cultural norm of individual teacher autonomy behind the classroom door. There is not a tradition of sharing data, conducting a diagnosis, taking action, and monitoring effects. The demands of external accountability, whereby not only do tests offer incomplete measures of performance but also teachers perceive external accountability as something that would or could be used against them, further hamper the development of decisional capital. Thus, the teaching profession has often fought against the open use of student data, either because it perceived the data to be misleading or out of fear districts would use it in inappropriate ways.

Despite these unfavorable conditions, districts that want to make a difference know they must establish an evidence-based culture. They buck the odds by deliberately pushing deeply into data to build decisional capital and fuel human and social capital, as seen in MGSD. In this chapter, we highlight the hallmarks of decisional capital and what it looks like to build it on a daily basis.

Hallmarks of Decisional Capital

The solution to improved performance in schools is tripartite capital—social, human, and decisional—in concert. To build decisional capital, MGSD systematizes the use of evidence, with four key conditions for embedding data (Edwards, 2014).

1. Accountability
2. Transparency and openness
3. Precision and speed
4. Data charts by school

Teacher leaders often talk about how "behind every number there is a child" to ensure accountability and put faces on the data. Students are brought into the picture as agents of their own monitoring:

> The kids like knowing how they're doing. They monitor their progress, and we discuss it. They've embraced their own accountability, and we have embraced ours. If anyone is not up to where they need to be, we can get the job done by analyzing our data together, and helping each other. We're a no-excuses team, and we know it. (Edwards, 2014, p. 119)

MGSD also works hard at establishing a culture of transparency, which does not come naturally to any organization. Transparency requires leaders to name, model, and monitor a culture of trust and precision about progress, and then employees can see the benefit. For example, a chapter titled "A Daily Date With Data," talks about ubiquitous access to formative student data, and how organizations should primarily use data to focus on instructional improvement (Edwards, 2014). Transparency is challenging at first, until people experience its value:

> This is my first year as a third-grade teacher. I knew you put up our names [alongside data on the performance of our students] and talked about us, and I thought it would be pretty intimidating, but now I can see it's about helping kids. (Edwards, 2014, p. 121)

Performance data transparency is explicitly named a valued practice at MGSD. "This means that teachers, grade-level chairs, departments, schools, and the district understand and accept that being open about the constructive use of data is a fundamental part of caring and our pedagogical approach" (Edwards, 2014, p. 126).

Precision and speed are also hallmarks of decisional capital, especially in relation to developing coherence (Fullan & Quinn, 2016):

> I'm doing the best teaching I've ever done. . . . We've learned to use digital resources to pinpoint intervention, so accuracy and precision have become a huge means for improvement. I could never go back to how I used to teach. It was a bunch of guessing and hoping. (Edwards, 2014, p. 70)

As this teacher experienced, precise and timely intervention is essential to move student learning forward. MGSD has seen a remarkable impact on students because of the immediate feedback on tests and assessments that digital tools provide, as well as the grade and school information instantly available in the district data system.

Collective data processing is important for every individual teacher. Team analysis of data requires grade levels or departments to study and reflect on the information (data) with intent to share success and problem solve together. At one data meeting, an MGSD kindergarten teacher summed up what was happening for her: "We bought into the concept of every child, every day, but these meetings [data charts by school] have really brought home to us that every teacher here has to accept responsibility for every child in the school" (Edwards, 2014, p. 121).

The daily preoccupation with data, action, and progress pays off in improved student achievement. Precision begets precision as well as additional pathways to better results. And the work is never done. At each MGSD school, teacher leaders have become skilled at using information to align instructional support to student needs, and their local leadership boosts the engine that drives student achievement. They help to analyze student formative data, implement instructional adjustments, and coach other staff.

As the work continues at MGSD, the district invests more and more deeply in the development of teachers and administrators who can lead data analysis to pinpoint and address learning needs for every student. Indeed, the work of building decisional capital is a day-by-day process.

Decisional Capital at the Day-to-Day Level

Effective school systems get to the point where, on any given day, they know how every student is doing. At the micro level, their data systems pinpoint with precision and speed how each student is doing. At the macro level, scores of individuals and groups use data every day to monitor progress and inform instruction.

Decisional capital is late to the educational table because in the past, schools could not gather and make precise data available. Pedagogical knowledge and new digital capabilities help address this problem. Also, new norms, skills, and ubiquitous leadership contribute to the deep cultural change essential for decisional capital to flourish. With social and human capital fueling it, once a decisional capital system gets going, schools see exponential growth and have opportunities to embed new systems and practices deeply into the culture.

The three capitals together and in interaction systematically circulate and implement on an ongoing basis what district staff are learning. (Refer to figure 3.1, page 32.) It is the combination and interaction of all three capitals that make the difference. Miss on any one of them, and the chances of improvement significantly decrease. Put the three in place as a synergistic set as MGSD did, and your district will flourish. It is this professional capital foundation that promotes and sustains continuous improvement and innovation.

chapter six

LESSONS FROM MGSD

Developing school systems for the modern age represents a huge challenge because most existing cultures are fundamentally ill suited for the new learning students require. However, the status quo is clearly dysfunctional, and deep change is called for. The excitement of the new learning provides the key to moving forward. Progress may be halting at first, but when the right elements come together, a set of forces comes into play with unstoppable momentum. We see this clearly in MGSD's accomplishments.

The big problem in the dissemination of good ideas is that you can't learn directly from successful cases. As much as we would like solutions to be handed to us on a platter, it is dangerous to accept them. Because each district and each school is unique, you must fully understand your own culture as the starting point, then look for insights from examples that seem successful, and finally adapt and formulate ideas as you start down your own learning pathway, being prepared to learn as you go. So, what can we learn from MGSD's success?

There are eight core lessons we can glean from MGSD's journey.

1. Secure the vision.
2. Build the culture.
3. Determine digital resources.
4. Develop capacity (to gain professional capital).
5. Focus on instructional design.
6. Cultivate coherence.
7. Confront distractors (to manage politics and policies).
8. Align resources (for sustainability).

It is critical that your own school district's journey adhere to these lessons, which requires short- and long-term attention. Because this is a complex work of collective will and deep, shared convictions, missing on even one or two of these items can cause the effort to fail. For example, if you have a strong stated vision but don't build the culture, it will remain a paper product. If you align resources but fail to focus on developing instructional expertise, the resources will be squandered. Let's take a closer look at each of these lessons.

Secure the Vision

Securing a vision starts with a multifaceted conversation that includes staff, students, parents, and community members. The initial dialogue is all about asking, "Why?" MGSD focused first on the moral imperative and what we wanted for students, linked to equity of opportunity for all students and all families.

MGSD also stressed the importance of instructional practices that would prepare students for their future. The goal was to ensure that teachers and students have the tools and resources that would enable them to do their best work.

This vision work is the cornerstone of social capital. It can be messy and take time. It may require several community meetings to work through potential hiccups and reach a consensus that the vision is about success for all students and teachers. MGSD held regular planning meetings for six months before embarking on a limited deployment.

The MGSD educational vision is also an economic vision for the community, because communities that have thriving education systems usually also enjoy thriving economies. Mooresville economic development leaders emphasize that a high-quality school district is a key dynamic in recruiting businesses. As EarthKind, Inc. CEO Kari Warberg Block said of her business's Mooresville expansion, "As a fast-growing business with a sustainable focus, we selected Mooresville due to the high quality of life and schools, plus to better serve our growing customer base" (Elkins, 2014).

In 2016, Mooresville approved over one thousand homes for construction, and real estate developers point to MGSD and its digital conversion as an attraction for potential homebuyers (Town of Mooresville Finance Department, 2016).

Build the Culture

A strong cultural foundation is essential for success in any district. A cultural foundation starts with defining beliefs and daily practices, like the following, and tying them together with how we treat each other and what we do together.

- Ensure that every member of the school community believes in and has high expectations for every student.
- Treat each other with kindness and respect.
- Develop the understanding that sharing and working together as adults are the best ways to teach students how to work together.

- Embrace personal and team accountability to connect social capital and human capital, and move toward decisional capital.
- Create a team of tenacious learners and voracious collaborators who deeply believe in what they are doing.

Superintendents, district leaders, principals, and teacher leaders must model, articulate, and establish the cultural norms day by day and hour by hour. They must demonstrate and lead a collaborative culture of caring that supports all stakeholders. Figure 6.1 displays the powerful recipe framework for growth that forms the essence of MGSD's culture.

Recipe for: MGSD culture

INSTRUCTIONS:

Start with a collaborative culture of caring.

Add high expectations.

Include data-informed and aligned lessons.

Include personalization.

Apply maximum efficacy.

Maximize all resources.

Cultivate reflection to grow and learn.

Figure 6.1: Elements of the MGSD culture.

We have seen throughout the previous chapters the MGSD's recipe in action. They work in concert and, as such, constitute Mooresville's culture of learning. Building school and district culture takes time and effort, and identifying key ingredients that serve as institutional sign posts helps establish the norms that influence the daily work.

Determine Digital Resources

Determining the technical infrastructure should follow this four-step sequence, with careful attention to each decision.

1. Build a robust network with ample bandwidth, filtering resources, and other safety elements.

2. Select devices to provide one-to-one access for every student and instructional staff member. Target a device that provides tools for students to build out multimedia projects, as well as presentation resources that support innovation and creativity.

3. Select a learning management system that provides a platform and repository for teacher and student work; a network for collaboration and research; and a communication channel for parents.

4. Select in-depth digital content that provides functionality and allows for personalized information in real time to empower students and teachers. Have teacher grade-level and content-area teams recommend digital content choices.

By adhering to this sequence, you can safeguard against making bad technology investments that deplete your resources without tangible benefits. There are ample data from efforts over the years that districts can use to ensure that all elements of the technology infrastructure are on solid footing. CoSN (www.cosn.org), Digital Promise (www.digitalpromise.org), and Project RED (http://one-to-oneinstitute.org) all provide source data related to planning for technical infrastructure.

Develop Capacity

It is crucial to take the long view when hiring and developing staff. Staff must be of the highest quality and embrace and own the culture, something that doesn't happen in districts engaged in short-term thinking. To take the long view, districts must do the following.

- Invest heavily in developing staff to build their individual capacity.
- Focus on the skills and dispositions that help people collaborate and work well as teams.
- Provide constant and evolving professional development to build decisional capital.
- Promote the need for continuous learning and reflection.

The new pedagogy of collaboration, inquiry, project work, and personalization will grow as individuals and teams develop the capacity to lead instruction in the new environment that builds authentic relevance to students' world today and their future tomorrow.

Improved indicators of student and teacher success will result. It is important to look at a wide range of indicators that respond to both inherent needs and public accountability demands, and function as a catalyst for improvement.

Focus on Instructional Design

Districts should be confident that they will grow into the new instructional model, although it will take time, energy, patience, persistence, and practice. Effective collaboration among students and staff requires skill and sustained attention. These skills include engaging students in collaborative inquiry, working effectively in teams, accessing and using external resources, using diagnostic assessment and corrective action relative to how well students are doing, and so on. As teachers move from a didactic framework to become facilitators and collaborators, they will need support, direction, and nurturance. Building collaborative expertise among students and teachers is central to getting to the deep learning and stratospheric pedagogical model that we advocate. Developing the capacity to collaborate requires intentional support of sharing, listening, and using interdependent working skills.

A comprehensive and well-thought-out instructional design that aligns with the new digital and pedagogical foundations is an evolving priority for all instructional leaders. Early signs of success will precede the glow of collaborative expertise that truly lights up teaching and learning. One of the real challenges is for a teacher to move toward a participatory culture where students help lead the instructional process by sharing what and how they are learning and what it means to them. For teachers, letting student voice become the main voice of the class requires deft orchestral skills.

At MGSD, instructional design has evolved organically since 2008, including the framework recipe depicted in figure 6.1 (page 60).

Cultivate Coherence

Fullan and Quinn (2016) say that coherence amidst the constant churn of initiatives and politics is the most difficult thing to accomplish in today's complex society. This is because coherence is fully and only *subjective*—if it doesn't exist in the minds of people (or if it is only on paper), for all intents and purposes it does not exist. Fullan and Quinn (2016) go one step further and conclude that *shared coherence* is essential. Their formal definition of coherence is "the shared depth of understanding about the purpose and nature of the work" (pp. 1–2). Single meetings, workshops, and episodic gatherings will not be intensive enough to develop shared coherence. Only focused interaction, day after day, with a common purpose, tested action, use of data, reflections, and corrections will be powerful enough to develop shared coherence. This is what we mean when we say *learning is the work*.

Since the goal of the work is to improve teaching and learning, communities want to see the improvement in several ways. In addition to engagement and creativity, they want to see improved student and school performance indicators, because public education requires that students, teachers, schools, and districts be held accountable.

Teachers and leaders, as well as students and parents, must be empowered with precise information about learning progress and needs. Creating the decisional capital to profitably use this information requires much development and refinement. This process is the toughest part of digital and pedagogical transformation because it requires going into detail and coming out with collective clarity.

MGSD wholeheartedly embraces transparency and uses data on graduation rates, attendance, scholarships, and citizenship, as well as on state assessments and college and career readiness, as ongoing examples of progress. School-level teams meet each quarter and engage in analysis and dialogue about formative indicators. This work fine-tunes and focuses the effort for the next quarter, providing the macro decisional capital essential for individual and team success.

Digital resources and collaborative opportunities should enhance every aspect of school life. At MGSD, all cocurricular offerings, including visual and performing arts, sports and athletics, and clubs and organizations use digital resources to great benefit.

Confront Distractors

The bane of focused innovation is constant diversions and ad hoc demands. Thus, effective districts like MGSD learn to stay the course (come hell or high water). Partly, they do this by developing and constantly updating policies and protocols, and ensuring that those they govern have input on these documents. The documents become alive through constant use. District leaders and teachers must work in concert with school boards as well as parents and community leaders to develop clear and effective policies. For example, the district annually updates the MGSD Technology Responsible Use Policy with input from the parent advisory committee and teaching staff. This policy includes sections on the following.

- Expectations for use of technological resources
- Rules for use of technological resources

- Identification of restricted Internet material
- Guidelines for parental consent
- Guidelines for privacy
- Rules for use of personal technology
- Best practices for security and care on property

Similarly, discipline policies need to align with the new ubiquitous technology, and job descriptions need to align with the new performance expectations. Policies, job descriptions, and daily dialogue must include the requirement that all staff embrace their own development. Such policies and protocols—because they are visible, used daily, and linked to other key elements (the coherence factor)—serve to reinforce the focus.

Align Resources

Although MGSD is one of the lowest-funded districts in North Carolina, the district has gone through three refreshes, with new machines, since 2008. A digital conversion requires a long-term commitment and prioritized resources. Districts must build long-term thinking into the operating budget and help their communities understand why.

MGSD stopped buying textbooks in 2010, and digital content purchases align with district goals and available financial resources. Districts must consider digital content purchases carefully and develop a go-to list of preferred resources.

Aligning resources for sustainability also requires an all-in commitment. The district should respect and enlist every employee, as well as every parent and every student, in the total effort. For example, MGSD bus drivers and custodians also serve as mentors and tutors for students after receiving basic training. MGSD's all-in effort has evolved and added real value, creating cultural conditions where all employees are not only respected and honored but also asked to strive to be the very best at what they do. Referring to this specifically as an *all-in effort* reinforces the belief that it is incumbent on everyone to help lift everyone else.

Collaborative synergy also serves sustainability. Once the engines of change start cranking, the enthusiasm for the new dynamic culture of learning and teaching will create a wave of new work, new learning, and new success. It is important to not only celebrate progress but also to avoid declaring premature victory. A deliberate effort to recognize emerging synergies creates new synergy, while building teams requires practice, attention, encouragement, and a sustained focus.

Another factor that reinforces and propels sustainability is continuous success itself, but not by itself. Communicate and celebrate good news. MGSD teachers constantly recognize their colleagues' leadership in their daily work. Principals, district leaders, and community leaders offer encouragement and talk about specific examples of their colleagues' initiative and effort. Students and staff are recognized every month at school board meetings, and an instructional highlight exemplifies the work and the progress, as well as the challenges. The school board constantly offers encouraging words to students and staff.

MGSD students hear from teachers and staff who recognize them and acknowledge their efforts and attitudes all the time. The transformation of social and human capital has been partly due to the daily dialogue about staying true to goals and beliefs. The emphasis is always on a strong efficacious disposition by all adults for all students, as they depend on each other to achieve short- and long-term goals, and to celebrate the independence of personalized work and the value of sharing and collaborating.

Dean Shareski (2017) captures the power of thoroughly engaging learning cultures in his book, *Embracing a Culture of Joy*:

> Engaging learning environments are naturally joyful places. These are places where . . . pursuing personal interests is expected. . . . Joyful learning is something even our youngest learners understand and

experience. . . . Those students who wake up each morn-
ing excited to go to school may indeed be going to a
place where joy is the dominant culture. (p. 16)

The next phase will be telling, as MGSD Superintendent Mark A. Edwards resigned in 2016 after almost ten years to take a position with a digital company. His successor is an internal appointment, former Executive Director of Secondary Education Stephen Mauney. As an internal leader, Mauney has been steeped in the development of the existing culture. In Fullan's (2016) *Indelible Leadership: Always Leave Them Learning,* he concludes that effective leaders should spend their energies developing collaborative cultures and other leaders for six or more years—to the point where they themselves become dispensable. This is what Edwards has attempted to do, especially in the last half of his tenure as superintendent. We asked new Superintendent Mauney what he thought of the situation as he begins his term. We see in the following account a sense of what he faces in the next phase of MGSD's evolution.

With change in leadership comes uncertainty about the future goals, expectations, and mission of the organization. This uncertainty is a natural response and a challenge that new leaders must recognize and combat. The Mooresville Graded School District experienced significant change at the school and district leadership levels prior to the beginning of the 2016–2017 school year. Eight schools make up the MGSD. Of these eight schools, five have new principals who have been in their current positions for two years or less. At the district level, the MGSD has either replaced or reassigned five of its eight-member executive team: the superintendent, the assistant superintendent for secondary instruction, the assistant superintendent for elementary instruction, the chief operations officer, and the director of technology. During this change, however, one important thing remains consistent: we maintain a culture of caring, conviction, and accountability.

When Mark Edwards first came to the MGSD, he brought with him plans for the well-known digital conversion, which leveled the digital playing field for all students through the one-to-one laptop initiative. He also brought to the district an increased focus on the use of

continued ➜

individual student performance data to drive instructional decision making and further develop individual and collective accountability related to student achievement. These two points of emphasis helped improve the quality of teaching and learning within the district and fostered the growth of the caring, student-centered culture evident in the district's motto, "Every child, every day."

One true measure of effective leadership is the ability of a leader to build other strong leaders within the organization who can carry out the organization's mission and continue the good work even after the leader leaves the organization. The MGSD devoted much time and effort in developing leadership skills of individuals at all levels of the organization: support staff, teachers, school-based administrators, and district administrators. Because of this development plan and the pervasive culture throughout the district, the great work going in the MGSD will continue.

The MGSD is a great place. The dedicated staff, committed students, and extremely supportive community allow the culture of caring, conviction, and accountability to flourish. This culture bridges the change in leadership and will enable the district to continue to perform at high levels. The staff truly care about their students and hold one another accountable to create and deliver high-quality, engaging lessons. The individuals in the district are committed to working together as a team to best serve our students and community. (S. Mauney, personal communication, September 26, 2016)

We see in this account a clear and deep affirmation of the MGSD culture. Once key ideas and habits are steeped in the organizational culture, they plant the seeds for generating innovative and compatible leaders well into the future. We believe for reasons stated throughout this book that MGSD is such an enduring culture. Continuous innovation within a framework of core values and effective practices is the key.

chapter seven

EMERGING MODELS

We have said that no district can successfully borrow solutions from others. However, a strong understanding of your own culture, combined with interaction from a successful culture, can stimulate good ideas. In this chapter, we look at a half-dozen U.S. districts distinguished for systematic attempts to establish the kind of learning-based, digital culture we have seen in Mooresville, each using its own distinctive design flavor. We look at the Houston Independent School District, the seventh largest U.S. district, as a mega, urban-district model. We also examine Wasatch County School District in Utah; East Irondequoit Central School District in New York; and Spartanburg School District 7 in South Carolina, all districts similar in size to MGSD but each unique in its own challenges and strengths. Finally, we look at two large urban-suburban districts, Baltimore County Public Schools in Maryland and Virginia Beach City Public

Schools, both well into their own digital conversions. These two districts have sent teams to Mooresville to engage in deep dialogue and study with MGSD staff to leverage collegial sharing and learning, and to inform and inspire their local efforts to create their digital and pedagogical models.

The range of these districts, as you're about to read, shows that any district can move down the pathway of pedagogically driven, digitally accelerated success if they focus on the core ideas we present in this book. All excuses are off the table!

Southwest: Houston

Houston Independent School District is the only large urban district that we know of to successfully power up digital use in the service of learning. Former Superintendent Terry Grier, who retired in 2016, led Houston ISD schools for seven years and, during his tenure, led one of the most successful large digital transformation programs in the United States. The Houston ISD PowerUp initiative (www.houstonisd.org/powerup) was both ambitious and inspiring for a mega-urban district. All high school students received a laptop computer for home and school use. All staff received comprehensive and sustained professional development to build the foundation for supporting staff and student learning.

We quote in detail then-Superintendent Grier's approach:

When I became superintendent of the Houston Independent School District in September 2009, I was immediately struck by the number of inequities that existed in the system. Schools in one part of town had wrought iron fencing surrounding their schools that would make you think you were driving into a private school or nice apartment complex. In other neighborhoods, the fencing around schools was rusted, broken, and framed with razor wire. Only three of the forty-five high schools offered three or more advanced placement courses. . . .

A more perplexing and complex inequity was the quality of teachers that worked in various schools across the district. To be clear, there were truly remarkably talented teachers in *all* Houston ISD schools. However, the density of those teachers differed greatly across the system. When a school in an affluent neighborhood had a fourth-grade opening, over one hundred teachers would appear at a job fair with applications in hand. At that same job fair, a school in a low socioeconomic part of town would only have one or two applicants for their fifth-grade opening. The chances of a poor child receiving a highly effective teacher for three years in a row was zero. . . . Realizing that you cannot fire yourself to greatness, we decided to turn to coaching our teachers to become facilitators of learning and to abandon textbooks in favor of teacher-developed, rigorous curricula that would engage students in real-life project-based learning experiences.

[In 2013], we started at the high school level and used technology as the driver to bring about a dramatic shift in how and what our teachers taught. It began by conducting benchmarking trips across the county to observe districts that declared they had made a digital conversion to manage and direct instruction. I attended most of the trips, and we included school board members, principals, teachers, and business leaders. What we learned from all but one district (after we removed the noise and smoke and mirrors) was what we did *not* want to do.

The last district we visited was the Mooresville Graded School District. . . . They realized it was not about the machines. Laptops were simply a tool to help teachers facilitate learning that engaged and motivated students to learn real-world skills and to ensure they were college or career ready.

Following our trips and numerous telephone and Skype conferences, we quickly found that there was not a tried-and-proven digital transformation model that had been successfully implemented in a large, urban school district in America. In fact, it was seeing these unsuccessful success stories and [then] visiting Mooresville that convinced us and our board that we could get a digital transformation right.

The board approved our program and adopted a budget to support our efforts. PowerUp [www.houstonisd.org/powerup] was born.

continued ➔

Drawing heavily on what we learned in Mooresville, we decided to eat our elephant a little bit at a time. We started with eleven high schools in year one, eighteen in year two, and sixteen in year three. And rather than partner with for-profit vendors, we decided to take an entrepreneurial approach in developing our training and curriculum development programs. We decided not to purchase any high school textbooks and to redirect those dollars toward lease-purchasing laptops and to support our curriculum development needs.

Houston ISD is the seventh largest school district in the United States, serving over 216,000 students in a diverse, urban environment. Many people were surprised and shocked when we decided to use Mooresville (with approximately 5,500 students, teachers, and administrators) to provide the bulk of our staff development training. Even members of our school board, who had made the trip to Mooresville to see their program, questioned the decision. After all, what could the staff of a small, primarily suburban school district with one high school know about the needs of the seventh largest school district in the country that had forty-five high schools? Well, as it turned out, they knew a lot.

We gave out our laptops to the teachers in our first eleven high schools in the summer of 2014. Mooresville teachers and administrators spent the summer training teachers. Rather than teaching about how to operate laptop computers, they taught our staff how to schedule schools to ensure common planning time; how to conduct group and course planning meetings; how to design a curriculum that was engaging and rigorous; and how to empower teachers and students to lead a digital transformation.

We allowed those eleven high schools to dismiss early, [with] students leaving immediately after lunch one day per month during the first semester of that year. Students were given their laptops at the beginning of the second semester in mid-February. We assigned a tech-savvy student leader to each teacher's classroom. Most were already students in the class. This distributive leadership helped give teachers who initially struggled with technology a feeling of comfort.

In year two [2015], teachers from those eleven schools joined the Mooresville team in leading our staff development efforts. At first blush, everything seemed to be progressing according to plan. . . .

You can imagine how surprised I was when several weeks later, a small group of high school principals told me that they had serious concerns about PowerUp's effectiveness. They said too little was being done to address their teachers who refused to attend training sessions, and their teachers were struggling to develop digital content. When I doubled back to our technology team, they denied this was happening and demanded to know the names of the principals.

Instead of giving names, we decided to have a third party come in and conduct an implementation audit. A team from the Mobile Technology [Learning Center] lab at the University of San Diego visited schools and held focus group meetings with teachers, administrators, and students. What they found should not have surprised us. We were given very high marks for the rollout portion of the program—distributing machines to teachers and students, and so on. School staffs felt our central office team provided excellent technical support when machines broke or the Internet went down. The University of San Diego audit team also reported that approximately 30 percent of our teachers were early adopters, 50 percent were on the fence, and 20 percent were digging in their heels.

Principal leadership was quickly identified as a key influence in PowerUp's success. Where we had a strong, whatever-it-takes leader, the program flourished. And, where we had a weak principal, there was less staff buy-in, bitter complaining, and little or no change in how or what teachers taught.

Rather than point fingers or assign blame, we quickly brought our central office staff, the Mooresville trainers, the University of San Diego auditors, and small teams from each of our high schools together to review the findings and to develop strategies to correct the identified deficiencies.

One of the first and most important decisions was to increase the amount of training for our principals and to be clear that if principals would not or could not lead the digital transformation in their schools, they would be reassigned. . . .

Once our principals got their schedules right—for example, all biology teachers in a school had the same planning period and were required to plan their lessons together—immediate improvement and increased buy-in occurred. Teachers were taught how to design

continued ➜

digital material, and our platform was used for teachers to share lessons and to engage in chats about what worked.

We continued the same process of summer distribution of equipment to teachers, second-semester distribution to students, [and] summer and ongoing first-semester staff development training, into year three [2016]. We doubled down on second-semester teacher and principal training. And, in the true spirit of distributive leadership, we added student assistants in each teacher's classroom. These very talented young people were tremendously helpful to our reluctant implementers. We stressed to our central office and school teams that good educational leaders do not make excuses, do not play the blame game, do not wait for permission to act, do not put things off, and do not quit.

You have not read or heard of the stop-start, stop-start, stop implementation problems in Houston that occurred in other major districts across the country. . . . Was the work easy? No. It was tough and continues to be a challenge. Did we have detractors? Yes. Change is hard, and often the people you think will present the most opposition are the most supportive and vice versa. The training is relentless and it will never go away, nor should it. Every year brings new teachers and school leaders and the opportunity to positively change the lives of children.

Laptops and other digital equipment are just that. It's all equipment. Digital conversion is *not* about the equipment; it is a fundamental change in how and what we teach our children. It is total commitment to quality training and adult development.

Two things are significant in the Houston ISD case. First, a big district can learn from a small successful district if they focus on the core concepts of building a learning culture that specifically addresses pedagogy and [the] capacity of principals and teachers. Second, each district must start with its own existing culture and reshape it accordingly. But the basic concepts are the same in all successful cases: it is about establishing engaging pedagogy linked to measurable impact, and the related capacity of adults to work collaboratively toward deeper learning never before achieved. (T. Grier, personal communication, September 20, 2016)

One of the lessons learned from the PowerUp Initiative in Houston ISD was the power of collaboration to scale for replication. The Houston ISD and MGSD teams grew together and developed a collegial trust that spurred reciprocal learning. Houston ISD leaders had the confidence to embrace learning from sharing with others, and it resulted in one of the most successful large district digital implementations in the country.

West: Utah

Wasatch County School District in Heber City, Utah, is a rural district nestled in the tops of the Wasatch Mountains east of Salt Lake City. It is the clear leader in Utah for digital conversion. Superintendent Paul Sweat is a thoughtful and determined leader who brought his leadership team members to Mooresville to immerse them in the culture and focus on student achievement. Wasatch provides all students, grades 2–12, with a personal laptop and all teachers with job-embedded professional development, along with sustained efforts to build strong school cultures. The district is intentionally raising the bar for student and teacher success through digital and pedagogical transformation.

As Wasatch uses lessons from Mooresville to craft its own vision, it identifies the following four critical components essential to its own district.

1. Viable digital curriculum
2. Job-embedded professional development and coaching
3. Digital-friendly classrooms
4. Digital devices for every student

Together, these components create a comprehensive digital learning foundation on which the district can build. The following sections each take a deeper look at these components.

Viable Digital Curriculum

Instead of tasking teachers with transforming existing curricula into a digital format, Wasatch completed an extensive search to identify the most current digital curriculum aligned with district standards. This kept the teachers' focus on improving their digital pedagogy rather than using valuable time altering existing curricula. This decision expedited the digital conversion process and allowed teachers to focus on the more important task of teaching and student learning.

Job-Embedded Professional Development and Coaching

Wasatch determined that an effective digital learning transformation would require professional development for individual teachers. The district placed a dedicated digital instructional coach in every school. The digital coaches are dedicated members of the school faculty and serve as important liaisons between vision and practice. These coaches were invaluable at the onset in helping teachers overcome fear and start down the path of digital instruction. In subsequent years, it became clear that the more important role of the coaches was to continually transform teaching and learning in each classroom.

Digital-Friendly Classrooms

Wasatch equipped each classroom in every school with projector technology that transformed existing whiteboards into interactive SMART Boards. In addition, the school utilized enhanced sound systems, wireless Internet access in each classroom, and up-to-date teacher laptops so each teacher and student had the tools necessary to succeed.

Digital Devices for Every Student

Wasatch implemented a strategic system to select the most appropriate digital device for each student. The system ensured that the student laptops allowed teachers to utilize new digital pedagogical approaches that promote collaboration and inquiry. Not only did the devices have to conform to the teachers' needs but also support ever-evolving software and curricula to enhance digital instruction.

Instead of seeing students seated in rows passively listening to a teacher lecture, in Wasatch you see busy student-centered classrooms where students use technology to accomplish learning goals based on a much deeper level of knowledge. Superintendent Sweat attributes increased levels of student learning to the district's digital initiative: "Instead of emphasizing remembering and understanding, we are now more focused on analyzing, evaluating, and creating" (P. Sweat, personal communication, August 26, 2016). Students in the district now engage in learning activities previously thought inconceivable.

North: New York

The East Irondequoit Central School District is one of twenty school districts in the Rochester, New York, area. It has emerged as a digital conversion leader since 2013, with Superintendent Susan Allen and Chief Information Officer Joe Sutorius leading the way. Allen, the 2016 New York State School Superintendent of the Year, sent teams to Mooresville from 2013 to 2015 to study the MGSD model from culture to achievement. East Irondequoit also contracted Mooresville leaders to provide training in Rochester. While East Irondequoit readily acknowledges that it used specific elements of the Mooresville model, it also built a very strong model of its own and has hosted a large and successful Digital Conversion Symposium that draws attendees from school districts across New York State. There is growing excitement and energy in East Irondequoit, and for good reason. According to Superintendent Allen:

In 2012–2013, East Irondequoit began researching more thoughtful ways to use instructional technologies across their district. Of particular interest were districts that had experience with one-to-one device implementations. . . . During their very first Mooresville visit, they were inspired by the focus and passion for this work the Mooresville staff exuded. It lit a spark in the East Irondequoit team that soon became a flame, and now has become a torch. As of November 2016, East Irondequoit has had over sixty-five districts visit them to learn about their work with digital conversion. Everyone who visits hears that East Irondequoit did not invent any of this, but instead discovered the blueprint for this in Mooresville, and that Mooresville is very willing to share. . . .

As East Irondequoit was preparing to roll out their first one-to-one device pilot [in 2013], there was much discussion about how to get teachers invested in this work. The East Irondequoit team had talked to districts that deployed devices to an entire school or grade level at a time, and then discovered that there were teachers included in those groups that were simply unwilling to embrace the change. So, what approach could be taken to get buy-in from all teachers in the pilot and help build an energized core group of teachers to inspire other teachers? The answer: proposals. The East Irondequoit team created a proposal document and announced that any teacher could complete and submit one if he or she wanted to be included in the device pilot. They [the teachers] would have to agree to meet at least quarterly to discuss progress and challenges and answer short periodic surveys. A selection committee was formed to evaluate the submissions and choose which teachers would be included. There were thirty-five proposals, submitted from fifty-four teachers (some of them submitted proposals together), and from these proposals we selected sixteen teachers.

Within ten weeks, the East Irondequoit team knew the proposal approach had worked, if for no other reason than the increased level of interest and engagement from every one of the sixteen pilot teachers and their students. The decision was made to announce that proposals were being accepted to expand the device pilot the following spring [of 2014], after which we received twenty-eight more proposals from forty-two teachers.

Fast forward to late spring. An announcement was made that proposals would be accepted for the following school year. Proposals were submitted that included 176 teachers (the district has a total of 312 teachers), which caught the team completely off guard! No one on the team expected that kind of response and, although it was a good problem to have, in the context of trying to create excitement and interest, the district simply could not expand the pilot that quickly. Many teachers were asked to be patient and told that the district was now committed to getting devices to every teacher and student.

During this whole time frame [2013–2016], some very wonderful things were happening with some of the East Irondequoit teachers. Most of the teachers in the very first pilot group became comfortable using devices in their classrooms. They had also been to many quarterly meetings to discuss progress and challenges, where they heard repeatedly that it was okay to be a risk taker and try new approaches to teaching with these devices and that they had the full support of the district. . . .

All sixteen teachers, their principals, and some administrators attended Summer Connection 2015 in Mooresville. A couple of these teachers heard that there would be an extracurricular event at a local bowling alley at the end of the first day, where each of the visiting districts were teamed up against each other. What do they do? They travel to a local Walmart and purchase twenty-six superhero T-shirts (with their own money) so everyone on the East Irondequoit team would be identifiable. Priceless! By the time this group of teachers returned to East Irondequoit, they were affectionately known as *the superheroes.*

The truth is, they really have become superheroes. Most of them were nominated by their principals to take part in a comprehensive multiyear digital learning professional development program offering called Digital Leader Corps (from Discovery Education). Through this program, these teachers learned how to be digital leaders for their peers and have agreed to offer encouragement and support for the other teachers in their schools. Many of these digital leader teachers (now twenty-eight strong) routinely offer professional development through the Office of Instruction to teachers around the district. They

continued ➜

also provide professional development during breakout sessions at the Digital Conversion Symposium hosted in East Irondequoit each year. This is an event open to any district that wants to learn about digital conversion. In November 2016, there were 198 attendees at the symposium, representing forty-nine school districts from New York State and Pennsylvania.

It's difficult to shift a culture, and therefore it is so rewarding to see evidence that it is happening. During the symposium in November 2016, there was a panel of teachers and administrators answering questions from the attendees. One of the teachers on this panel was part of the very first pilot group of sixteen teachers and teaches fifth grade. The question, asked by someone from the audience, was, "How do you handle student device technical issues that arise while you are teaching?"

Without hesitation, this teacher responded that she identifies students in her class who are experts with devices and apps and designates them as *tech titans*. When an issue arises, she simply asks one of her titans to tackle it. Sometimes she doesn't even ask; the titans often respond before she does. What a great opportunity for these students to contribute, to feel a sense of ownership, and perhaps a twinge of leadership.

East Irondequoit has also been fortunate to bring a team of Mooresville teachers and administrators to the district to work directly with the East Irondequoit digital leader teachers. It was during their second visit, in the spring of 2016, that one of the Mooresville teachers made a comment that East Irondequoit was much further along in year two of its digital conversion than they were in theirs. In essence, they were saying that East Irondequoit was progressing more quickly than Mooresville had. Many East Irondequoit team members turned to each other in amazement because they had recently said the same thing about one of their neighboring districts that is also emulating this work. One might think that the rate of digital conversion progression in any given district will increase as more districts join the journey and share their work. . . .

The East Irondequoit leadership team is doing their best to convince East Irondequoit teachers that teaching can be a team sport. Teachers are encouraged to share their expertise with each other, build common assessments together, collaborate in professional learning communities, and even co-teach when possible. We all need to embrace this same philosophy with other districts. Digital conversion can also be a team sport. (S. Allen, personal communication, September 18, 2016)

As this story illustrates, East Irondequoit created a significant level of team synergy by focusing on culture as they began their initiative and had a strong drive to pave the way for transformation. When you see the East Irondequoit team's commitment to deep learning, you can sense the momentum.

Southeast: South Carolina

Superintendent Russell Booker's dynamic brand of leadership has propelled Spartanburg School District 7 in South Carolina into the U.S. spotlight. Early in his tenure as superintendent, he was interested in the achievements taking place in Mooresville, and eager to leverage MGSD successes for the benefit of his own students. From our first meeting with him in 2011, there was no doubt that Superintendent Booker and his team had begun to forge their own strategy.

Superintendent Booker and his team's successful digital initiative put mobile learning devices in the hands of every student in grades 3–12. The results are impressive, with outstanding achievement and development of pedagogical and cultural transformation for both students and faculty. The League of Innovative Schools, Apple, Inc., and Future Ready Schools cited District 7 in 2014 for its best-practice efforts in the implementation of one-to-one technology. The district is a huge advocate for collegial networking and collaborative learning and, in many ways, has followed MGSD's lead in providing guidance and mentoring to districts that seek expertise. Pointing to what Superintendent Booker calls the *audacity of inaction*, District 7's mandate to eliminate the digital divide was a rallying cry to level the playing field for every student in the district. Superintendent Booker notes:

Spartanburg School District 7 is a small urban school district located in the heart of upstate South Carolina. District 7 is a majority-minority district with a poverty index nearing 80 percent, a graduation rate of 84 percent, and a postsecondary enrollment rate that averages over 80 percent each year. It's often said throughout the community that the success and vitality of District 7 and the city of Spartanburg are inextricably bound together. In fact, our work with a broad range of community partners is rooted in that very recognition of connectivity, and serves as a catalyst in our shared commitment to quality education from cradle to career.

In District 7's earliest discussions about the importance of eliminating the digital divide, we concluded that leveling the playing field for our students was more than a good idea. Dr. [Mark A.] Edwards often spoke of this as a moral imperative, and we challenged the *audacity of inaction* with a bold decision to champion all our children. We placed an intentional focus on the hope, engagement, and well-being of our students—our new mission, vision, and values statement is a clarion call to ensure that in everything we do we "inspire and equip our students for meaningful lives of leadership and service as world citizens." Be it our commitment to digital learning, our attention to the curricula development in all our schools, the passage of a $185 million referendum that paves the way for dynamic new learning facilities, or the individual relationships we cultivate with our children and faculty, we are forging the charge to measure more than students' mastery of knowledge. We're fueling a culture and climate that support the whole child from the earliest stages of development well into the realization of his or her life's aspirations.

On a number of fronts where our presence at the table is tied directly to significant gains taking place in our community, it's exhilarating to see the pivotal role we play in the realization of collective impact. For example, our involvement in a blighted neighborhood on the north side of the city has been key to reviving a challenged elementary school in the district. In fact, through our affiliation with Purpose Built Communities [http://purposebuiltcommunities.org] and the Northside Development Group [www.spartanburgndg.com], District 7's investment in the Cleveland Academy of Leadership [then one of the highest-poverty elementary schools in the district] has brought about tremendous gains for the families living in this section of Spartanburg and increasing achievement scores for our students at Cleveland. On a similar note, in affiliation with several educational entities, the district's Advanced Placement and [Viking] Early College programs are enjoying tremendous growth and providing a host of college-readiness opportunities for the youth in our community. . . .

To further our commitment to early learning, the district forged a unique public-private partnership this year with Meeting Street Academy in Spartanburg [www.meetingstreetacademy.com/Home .aspx]. Established initially as a private organization, Meeting Street Academy in Spartanburg is now a District 7 school, enabling us to expand three thousand offerings and provide our families with more options for school choice. Meanwhile, in a similar public-private partnership, our secondary students are immersed in early college dual-credit courses with the support of local colleges. Our Early College programs are designed to provide a direct path to higher education for students who might not otherwise have the resources to maximize their full potential. And while the list of cooperative projects like this continues to grow, perhaps the most impressive initiative launched with the help of our community is the district's one-to-one technology program, called *7Ignites* [http://7ignites .com]. District 7 has gained national visibility for its approach to blended teaching and learning and has essentially eliminated the digital divide.

As we guide our nation's schools, we (as educational leaders) will call greater attention to the needs of our students if we stand, and work, together. If we believe a dynamic and healthy school system is a powerful predictor of student success, then combining our resources and collaborating more fully will be a singular lynchpin in the promise of our collective and unstoppable momentum. When we talk about the good of the whole—let's focus on the good of the *whole child*. To support the power of partnership, let's remember that the strength of our individual relationships will enrich our collegial connections, and the unique needs and local challenges of our varied and various school systems should be a common call for excellence across the board. (R. Booker, personal communication, September 22, 2016)

District 7 represents the example of keeping the focus on student learning and building everything around it. Reaching out to the faith community to ensure student broadband access is a great example of solving problems with the community and for the community.

Mid-Atlantic: Maryland

Dallas Dance started the work of whole-system change almost immediately upon his arrival in 2013, when he began his tenure as superintendent of Baltimore County Public Schools (BCPS) in Maryland, a large urban-suburban district of over one hundred thousand students. Superintendent Dance, who resigned from the district in 2017, brought school board members, district and school leaders, and teachers to Mooresville and moved with great vigor to initiate a major digital conversion with a rollout spread over time for practical scaling. Superintendent Dance generated tremendous enthusiasm for the big digital and pedagogical transformation in the very large and complex school system. The BCPS cabinet team developed their unique design and focus with several key lessons and designs from many visits by many staff to Mooresville. As the district's chief communications officer, Mychael Dickerson, expresses:

Dallas Dance began his tenure as superintendent by listening to stakeholders from across BCPS, an urban-suburban school system where the enrollment [in 2016–2017] exceeds 112,000 students. The community's concerns about inequitable resources led to the Blueprint 2.0 [https:bcps.org/blueprint] strategic plan, which focuses on graduating every student [to be] globally competitive with access to an effective digital learning environment and second-language proficiency.

Team BCPS cabinet members, system and school leaders, and teachers visited Mooresville while designing the Students and Teachers Accessing Tomorrow (S.T.A.T.) [www.bcps.org/academics /stat] one-to-one transformation in teaching and learning. S.T.A.T. is redefining instruction in a blended learning environment with a digital curriculum, intensive professional learning, and a shift to learner-centered environments.

Visiting Mooresville as a team of leaders helped BCPS plan deliberately for implementation in a large, diverse, and growing school system. Keys to S.T.A.T.'s strong foundation include its equity focus, its intentional support structure, and its commitment to continuous improvement.

Equity drives the team BCPS approach, as the economy demands higher levels of skill and knowledge for college and career success. Educators leverage technology to enable personalized learning that helps every student grow every year.

The support structure is intentional. A digital curriculum, created by and for BCPS educators, and role-targeted professional learning preceded the selection of a digital device to emphasize instructional strategies necessary for effective, systemwide blended learning.

A S.T.A.T. teacher at every school coaches educators on facilitating learner-centered environments that deeply engage students and respond to individual needs. Infrastructure includes the BCPS One [https://bcpsone.bcps.org] digital ecosystem for educator and family access to learning systems, as well as wireless and broadband at every school and library.

[BCPS] Lighthouse schools [www.bcps.org/news/articles/article4477 .html] act as demonstration labs, the first in the county to place a device in the hands of students in selected grades. Lessons learned from these pioneering schools informed the one-to-one expansion to all elementary schools, and to Lighthouse secondary schools. The robust Lighthouse visitor program ensures insight and feedback from systems throughout the country.

Rounding out the continuous improvement process is transparent, public information about S.T.A.T.'s progress from an independent evaluation. The evaluation logic model explains how and when S.T.A.T. is expected to affect instructional practice and student achievement.

Learning from leaders, staff, and students on-site in Mooresville prepared BCPS to design S.T.A.T. as a sustainable transformation that is responsive to local needs and Blueprint 2.0. (M. Dickerson, personal communication, September 28, 2016)

As of 2017, BCPS is only at the front-end planning stage, and the effects of Dance's departure remain to be seen. However, during his tenure, the district was able to derive clear ideas from MGSD because it had prepared to seek pedagogical and digital solutions. BCPS is a large, complex school district, and its implementation's deliberate approach to ensure staff had time to build internal capacity makes a lot of sense. Working with the community to take it a step at a time, but with clear urgency for the greater mission, represents thoughtful leadership.

East: Virginia

Virginia Beach City Public Schools (VBCPS) is the third-largest district in Virginia and, with over eighty-eight thousand students, it is a diverse urban-suburban district. VBCPS Superintendent Aaron Spence, who also worked in Henrico with Mark Edwards, helped lead that district into the digital spotlight with a strong plan to build a districtwide digital conversion. Its initial implementation has been successful, creating excitement and energy with faculty, students, and the community. Although Superintendent Spence has led previous digital initiatives as a principal and superintendent, he still embraced the Mooresville model as a learning catalyst for the VBCPS team and sent teams to MGSD for its summer conference in 2014.

Superintendent Spence's comments to Mark Edwards about learning for growth, seeing is believing, and looking ahead, are germane to how a district that is primed to learn can rapidly gain ideas from others. Having worked at both Moore County, North Carolina, and VBCPS, he is also in a unique position to compare the two:

I've had experience integrating digital learning as a building principal and a district leader. I have the great fortune to consider Mark Edwards a key mentor, both as my superintendent when I was a principal in Henrico County [Public Schools in Virginia] and as a longtime colleague doing this work together. As I watched what he

[Edwards] and his team were accomplishing in Mooresville, it was clear that [my teams] needed to spend some time learning from them, and so I asked teams from Moore County, North Carolina, and [later] Virginia Beach to visit there, observe, and reflect on what was making such a difference for students. Through my own experiences and these times spent in Mooresville, I've learned two key lessons. First, know why you want to do this. Second, start small and build capacity—make sure the work you are doing matches the *why*, and make sure the people in your organization and community are ready to create that reality for your students.

It cannot be overstated how important it is that the entire community—including both internal and external stakeholders—understands why you are doing this before taking on digital learning on a broad scale. When you visit Mooresville schools and classrooms, it's clear what their *why* is. When you talk with teachers, school leaders, and even community members as you walk down Main Street, you understand without any question that student learning is the primary focus. There is a pervasive culture that kids come first and that the teachers and leaders there will do anything in their power to see that every student is successful. . . .

In both Moore County and in Virginia Beach, we also began by identifying our *why* rather than focusing on the digital tools themselves. In Moore County, we spent a lot of time talking about the need to engage students more fully in their learning if we were going to make a real difference in the learning environment. In relatively short order—largely because of visits by school and community leaders to Mooresville—it became clear that technology would be one way to accelerate this engagement. But the conversation was never about technology for technology's sake. In fact, almost immediately, we decided to stop talking about one-to-one initiatives and focus our conversations on digital learning, putting the emphasis on *learning*.

In Virginia Beach, fortunately, we had a good starting point when I arrived in 2014. That year, our district adopted a new strategic plan called Compass to 2020 [www.vbschools.com/compass/2020/landing.asp]. Stakeholder groups from across the city came together over the course of a year to create this plan. The plan highlights four main areas for improvement, and one of the key objectives outlined is the need to create a personalized learning environment for kids. Specifically, to address personalized learning needs, we state clearly

continued ➡

that we will "use digital learning as a pathway to personalized learning by increasing student flexibility with respect to when and how learning occurs." So, we began with a goal in mind that had been agreed upon by our board and our entire community.

We also believed in both districts that we couldn't just jump into a whole district initiative and be successful—we just weren't ready for it. We needed to start small, to learn together how technology could be used effectively in our classrooms to help us meet our goals around personalized learning, and to be prepared to share those lessons across schools and across the district. Our teachers and leaders would need to see that this would work to believe it could be effective in their classrooms.

In Moore County, we started with one school [in 2012], led by entrepreneurial Principal Denny Ferguson, and put iPads in every classroom. We used this as an opportunity to study the impact of these devices on kids and learning, and to understand some of the challenges of being a digital learning school from the perspective of our teachers, parents, and students. Importantly, we also used this school to showcase the impact technology in the classroom could have on student engagement—our stated *why*. Very quickly, we found enough reasons to believe this was the right approach for kids that the next year [2013] we launched a pilot program in several schools.

Similarly, in Virginia Beach, we identified a set of laboratory schools, which we've called our Digital Learning Anchor Schools [www.vb schools.com/curriculum/digitallearning] (anchoring us to best practices!). In year one [2015], eleven elementary, middle, and high schools participated as the first Anchor Schools. We identified these schools based on an application process, wherein we asked schools to sign onto capacity building and expectations for instructional practices that would reflect a more personalized learning experience for our students. Again, we wanted to study the extent to which technology could be integrated into our classrooms to support our *why*.

In both districts, success was not left to chance. The projects were and have been thoughtfully managed along the way, with key outcomes and expectations established early on for instruction, student learning, curriculum and resource development and access, and professional learning. Beginning with the end in mind allowed [both districts] to monitor and evaluate the field tests and pivot when needed. . . .

Importantly, leadership and support were not left solely in district hands. In both [districts], we established digital leadership teams that included leadership from the districts' technology teams and instructional teams, school leadership (including teachers), and key leaders within the broader community. The key function of these teams was to clearly define the *why* and establish metrics and anticipated outcomes. These teams also helped shape the future form of the digital transformation by providing sharp insight into what was happening in the buildings. For example, one of the key and interesting steps taken in both districts was to use different devices across these schools with the intention of monitoring which devices best support our teachers and students as they work to meet intended outcomes. Based on this, digital leadership teams in both districts were critical in providing their insights into how different devices helped or hindered student learning across different grade levels and content areas.

A sure sign of the success of these initiatives, which were celebrated in digital learning showcases at the end of each pilot cycle, is that the desire expressed by other schools to join the program grew rapidly and organically in both [Moore County and VBCPS].

Although I wasn't in Moore County to watch as that initiative took flight, I have had the chance to watch what's happening in Virginia Beach. As we look ahead in VBCPS toward expansion, this excitement has created its own challenges, and we've been forced to think through our readiness to expand both at the school and [district] levels. Our Chief Academic Officer Amy Cashwell has developed an impressive readiness rubric based on dispositions toward change, personalized learning, and technology to help with this.

As schools evaluate their own readiness, we're better able to identify who has the capacity to be added to the expanding program. And, importantly, we can work with those schools that are not quite ready to design a specific professional learning program that will help them achieve readiness, with a goal toward bringing on all schools as rapidly but as seamlessly as possible. (A. Spence, personal communication, September 18, 2016)

Leadership matters, and both Moore County and VBCPS have seen the benefits of a visionary leader who inspires a greater community vision for the district. Once again cultural foundations that promote deep efficacy for all students are the catalyst for instructional transformation.

Although we only reference a handful of districts in this chapter, it is exciting to see evidence that school districts from all over the United States are taking strong steps forward with thoughtful and courageous efforts to lead transformational work for teachers, students, and communities. Collaborative networks among educators are proving to be a new catalyst that compels growth for deep learning.

CONCLUSION

To put it negatively, we know one thing for sure—you cannot buy your way into the future by adding technology. If you start with technology, you end up going down that pathway. Pedagogy and culture drive change, and technology accelerates it—*if you get the sequence right.*

This book presents three powerful, positive lessons. First, there is an enormous appetite among districts to find out how to harness digital technology in the service of pedagogy and student learning. The message from us is to network, network, network—*with purpose.* On the same point, we see unequivocal evidence that districts are willing to share and learn from each other. This augurs well, as we need these ideas to proliferate across the whole system. Districts like MGSD are willing to share freely with any outsiders willing to learn. The fact that so many other districts are learning from MGSD and becoming successful validates Mooresville's success. And MGSD knows that it will become stronger by helping and learning from others. Indeed, districts more generally desire to work and learn in networks. This represents a powerful new system strategy called *leadership from the middle* (Fullan, 2015). The *middle* is districts, individually and together. The logic is that we need whole-system change (whole states or provinces and countries); that top-down change does not work; that bottom-up change is too fragmented; and that the best chance is for the middle (districts) to learn from each other and become better partners upward to the state or province and country (levels) and downward to individual schools.

We see plenty of evidence in the case of MGSD that our leadership from the middle strategy has huge potential for system change.

The second big lesson is that the substance of the change must consist of a certain specificity and quality. Among the key ingredients: digital technology is powerful, but only if it is an accelerator to pedagogy (the driver); new engaging pedagogy is essential, and we know increasingly what it looks like; collaborative focused culture is the sine qua non for effectiveness; evidence or data drives improvement; *everyone* must be involved (students, parents, community, classified staff, teachers, and administrators)—no exceptions; and leadership at all levels comes from all sources and is part and parcel of the necessary community change.

Third, in the Mooresville case, and more generally in our deep learning work, a remarkable finding is emerging that we call the *equity hypothesis*. There is evidence, and we are continuing to examine the data carefully, that deep learning is good for all, but it is *especially* effective for historically underserved students. MGSD—a district with significant poverty—proves that all students can learn regardless of background. Students most disconnected from traditional schooling find that the day-to-day relevance of new learning, its application to real problems, and its access to information all serve to stimulate and engage these students, who, for the first time, find themselves enjoying school success (Fullan, 2015). We will continue to pursue the equity hypothesis in our wider work.

One gets a sense that now is the moment. It is time for whole-system change, and MGSD is a tiny but critical indicator that deep change can be accomplished. At the same time, there is a huge upheaval occurring in the world, particularly in the United States, with regard to how federal education policy is changing following the 2016 presidential election. Never has it been more critical that students immerse themselves in the values and global competencies essential for living in an ever-complex universe. MGSD and the many districts like it have given us an encouraging start.

In light of all of this, we offer you one final piece of advice. The world needs you—join with others and be a player!

REFERENCES AND RESOURCES

Blume, H. (2014, August 25). LA Unified halts contract for iPads. *Los Angeles Times*. Accessed at www.latimes.com/local/education /la-me-deasy-ipads-20140826-story.html on March 15, 2017.

Boston Consulting Group. (2014). *Teachers know best: Teachers' views on professional development*. Washington, DC: Gates Foundation.

Cuban, L. (2013). *Inside the black box of classroom practice: Change without reform in American education*. Cambridge, MA: Harvard Education Press.

Edwards, M. A. (2014). *Every child, every day: A digital conversion model for student achievement*. Boston: Pearson.

Edwards, M. A. (2016). *Thank you for your leadership: The power of distributed leadership in a digital conversion model*. Boston: Pearson.

Elkins, K. (2014, September 22). Earth-Kind plans to grow to 380 employees at planned Mooresville facility. *Charlotte Business Journal*. Accessed at www.bizjournals.com/charlotte/blog /outside_the_loop/2014/09/earth-kind-plans-to-grow-to-380 -employees-at.html on March 10, 2017.

Every Student Succeeds Act (ESSA) of 2015, Pub. L. No. 114–95, § 114 Stat. 1177 (2015–2016).

Fullan, M. (2008). *The six secrets of change: What the best leaders do to help their organizations survive and thrive*. San Francisco: Jossey-Bass.

Fullan, M. (2010). *All systems go: The change imperative for whole system reform*. Thousand Oaks, CA: Corwin Press.

Fullan, M. (2013). *Stratosphere: Integrating technology, pedagogy, and change knowledge*. Toronto, Ontario, Canada: Pearson Education.

Fullan, M. (2014). *The principal: Three keys to maximizing impact.* Indianapolis, IN: Wiley.

Fullan, M. (2015). Leadership from the middle: A system strategy. *Education Canada, 55*(4), 22–26.

Fullan, M. (2016). *Indelible leadership: Always leave them learning.* Thousand Oaks, CA: Corwin Press.

Fullan, M., & Quinn, J. (2016). *Coherence: The right drivers in action for schools, districts, and systems.* Thousand Oaks, CA: Corwin Press.

Fullan, M., Quinn, J., & McEachen, J. (in press). *New pedagogies for deep learning: Leading transformations in schools, districts, and systems.* Thousand Oaks, CA: Corwin Press.

Gravelle, P. B. (2003). *Early evidence from the field: The Maine Learning Technology Initiative—Impact on the digital divide.* Accessed at https://usm.maine.edu/sites/default/files/cepare/MLTI_Impact_on_the_Digital_Divide.pdf on April 6, 2017.

Hargreaves, A., Boyle, A., & Harris, A. (2014). *Uplifting leadership: How organizations, teams, and communities raise performance.* San Francisco: Jossey-Bass.

Hargreaves, A., & Fullan, M. (2012). *Professional capital: Transforming teaching in every school.* New York: Teachers College Press.

Hattie, J. (2012). *Visible learning for teachers: Maximizing impact on learning.* New York: Routledge.

Hattie, J. (2015). *What works best in education: The politics of collaborative expertise—1 year input = 1 year progress.* London: Pearson.

Jenkins, L. (2013). *Permission to forget: And nine other root causes of America's frustration with education.* Milwaukee, WI: ASQ Press.

Leana, C. R. (2011). The missing link in school reform. *Stanford Innovation School Review, 9*(4), 30–35.

Mooresville Graded School District. (n.d.). *Summer connection.* Accessed at www.mgsd.k12.nc.us/page.cfm?p=2788 on April 6, 2017.

New Pedagogies for Deep Learning. (n.d.). *Deep learning competencies.* Accessed at http://npdl.global on April 6, 2017.

No Child Left Behind (NCLB) Act of 2001, Pub. L. No. 107–110, § 115, Stat. 1425 (2002).

North Carolina Department of Public Instruction. (n.d.a). *Reports and statistics*. Accessed at www.ncpublicschools.org/data/reports/ on March 17, 2017.

North Carolina Department of Public Instruction. (n.d.b). *Cohort graduation rates*. Accessed at www.ncpublicschools.org /accountability/reporting/cohortgradrate/ on March 17, 2017.

November, A. (2012). *Who owns the learning? Preparing students for success in the digital age*. Bloomington, IN: Solution Tree Press.

One-to-One Institute. (n.d.). *Introducing Project RED*. Accessed at http://one-to-oneinstitute.org/introducing-project-red on April 6, 2017.

Organisation for Economic Co-operation and Development. (2015). *Students, computers, and learning: Making the connection*. Paris: Author.

Schwarz, A. (2012, February 12). Mooresville's shining example (it's not just about the laptops). *New York Times*. Accessed at www.nytimes .com/2012/02/13/education/mooresville-school-district-a-laptop -success-story.html on April 6, 2017.

Sellers, D. (2002, November 14). Henrico schools win award for iBook program. *Macworld*. Accessed at www.macworld.com /article/1007785/henrico.html on April 6, 2017.

Shareski, D. (2017). *Embracing a culture of joy*. Bloomington, IN: Solution Tree Press.

Sheninger, E., & Murray, T. C. (2017). *Learning transformed: 8 keys to designing tomorrow's schools, today*. Alexandria, VA: Association for Supervision and Curriculum Development.

Solomon, B. (2014, March 27). 'Be right at the end of the meeting, not the beginning' - Honeywell's David Cote. Accessed at www.forbes.com/sites/briansolomon/2014/03/27/be-right-at-the -end-of-the-meeting-not-the-beginning-honeywell-chief-david -cote/#77143c624fec on January 11, 2017.

Town of Mooresville Finance Department. (2016). *Comprehensive annual financial report for the fiscal year ended June 30, 2016*. Accessed at http://ci.mooresville.nc.us/ArchiveCenter/ViewFile /Item/271 on April 7, 2017.

U.S. Department of Education. (n.d.). *ConnectED: Learning powered by technology.* Accessed at www.ed.gov/connected on April 6, 2017.

Williams, J. (2012, August 16). Fixing our schools—here are solutions that work. *Fox News.* Accessed at www.foxnews.com /opinion/2012/08/16/fixing-our-schools-solutions-that-work.html on April 6, 2017.

INDEX

Leadership
Lyle Kirtman and Michael Fullan
Develop a creative, productive school culture. Explore seven core leadership competencies for systemic change in schools, districts, and state education systems; discover targeted strategies to overcome initiative overload; and gain the know-how to create enjoyable, innovative learning environments.
BKF629

Change Wars
Edited by Andy Hargreaves and Michael Fullan
Michael Barber, Linda Darling-Hammond, Richard Elmore, Michael Fullan, Andy Hargreaves, Jonathan Jansen, Ben Levin, Pedro Noguera, Douglas Reeves, Andreas Schleicher, Dennis Shirley, James Spillane, and Marc Tucker
What can organizations do to create profound, enduring changes? International experts prove successful change can be a realistic goal and then explore constructive alternatives to traditional change strategies.
BKF254

Cultures Built to Last
Richard DuFour and Michael Fullan
Take your professional learning community to the next level! Discover a systemwide approach for re-envisioning your PLC while sustaining growth and continuing momentum on your journey. You'll move beyond pockets of excellence while allowing every person to be an instrument of lasting cultural change.
BKF579

Evaluating and Assessing Tools in the Digital Swamp
Michael Fullan and Katelyn Donnelly
Learn how the Digital Swamp Index can help educators wade through digital innovations to uncover tools that truly accelerate student achievement. Explore how to use the index to effectively address the revolution occurring in education, which is generating a new nature of learning.
BKF636

Wait! Your professional development journey doesn't have to end with the last pages of this book.

We realize improving student learning doesn't happen overnight. And your school or district shouldn't be left to puzzle out all the details of this process alone.

No matter where you are on the journey, we're committed to helping you get to the next stage.

Take advantage of everything from **custom workshops** to **keynote presentations** and **interactive web and video conferencing**. We can even help you develop an action plan tailored to fit your specific needs.

Let's get the conversation started.

Call 888.763.9045 today.

SolutionTree.com